"I'm eternally grateful to professional songwriters, the unsung heroes of many giant careers. Shelly Peiken provides fascinating insight into this least understood profession to the thorough delight of the reader."

—*Clive Davis*

"In the conversational tone of your BFF, Shelly Peiken tells you everything about the life of a songwriter. The good, the bad, the funny, the sad, what you need to know, what you want to know and even what you wish you didn't know, but are now grateful she told you. *Confessions of a Serial Songwriter* is the 'must have' songwriter's guide to life in the music business."

—*Cynthia Weil*

"Life, love and lyrics: with her open heart and personal prose, Shelly takes readers through the looking glass into one of the music industry's…most essential professions. Anyone aspiring to a career as a songwriter will find a wealth of eye-opening revelations and hard-won wisdom within these pages."

—*Dan Kimpel, Song Biz Editor, Music Connection Magazine*

"I relate to this strange, small world of which you speak—the games, the competition, the doubts, the sadness, the elation, the camaraderie, the 'songwriter's high'…seeking a better way. We are not alone."

—*Candice Beu, Mother and former Recording Artist on S-Curve Records*

"Shelly is a true beacon in the night for the rest of us."

—*Teresa LaBarbera Whites, A&R*

"Shelly brings authorial wisdom and a perpetual coolness to the pop song like no one else."

—*Greg Wells, Grammy-nominated Producer and Songwriter*

"Shelly bares her soul, speaks of her triumphs, her insecurities, her loves and her losses. On these pages you will see that her songs and her life are inseparable…her life is where her songs come from."

—*Kevin Cronin, REO Speedwagon*

"It is incredibly hard sometimes to earn respect in the writing room when you're a young singer-songwriter. Shelly, however, not only respected what I had to say, but also nurtured my ideas in such a caring way. After writing with her, I felt that I had both collaborated with her and learned a lot from her!"

—*Laura Marano, Actress, Recording Artist*

"Folks need to read and know about the great women in the music business."

—*Kevin Goins, Editorial Coordinator at SoulMusic.com*

"I love Shelly's ability to really tap into the personal and turn it into something catchy and sing-able in record time. She's such a warm, creative, caring person, who really invests herself in each song, and I've really enjoyed picking her brain about how to be a working songwriter and a mom at the same time."

—*Lisa Loeb, Recording Artist*

"Shelly Peiken gives even more meaning to this wacky world we're lucky enough (and crazy enough) to be a part of."

—*Emily Warren, Songwriter*

"Shelly's writings are some of the best I've ever read regarding this truly life-morphing process, always from a chef's stew of her own personal *and* professional senses. For those of us who share these wonderful yin yang days, weeks, years and/or decades searching for *the* note or *the* line or *the* mood or *the* sound that makes us go 'aah…'—capturing in those moments something we soooooo want to describe, but ultimately come up short of, she gets as close as anyone has a right to."

—*Mikal Paul, Musician*

CONFESSIONS
-of a-
SERIAL
songwriter

CONFESSIONS
-of a-
SERIAL
songwriter

SHELLY PEIKEN

Backbeat
Books
An Imprint of Hal Leonard Corporation

Peiken,
Shelly

Published in 2016 by Backbeat Books
An Imprint of Hal Leonard Corporation
7777 West Bluemound Road
Milwaukee, WI 53213

Trade Book Division Editorial Offices
33 Plymouth St., Montclair, NJ 07042

Permissions can be found on pages 270–275, which constitute an extension of this copyright page. Every reasonable effort has been made to contact copyright holders and secure permission. Omissions can be remedied in future editions.

Edited by Ronny S. Schiff

Cover Design and Formatting by Wicked Book Covers, www.wickedbookcovers.com

Cover Photography by Karen Ray Photography, www.karenrayphotography.com

Printed in the United States of America.

Library of Congress Cataloging-in-Publication Data

Names: Peiken, Shelly.
Title: Confessions of a serial songwriter / Shelly Peiken.
Description: Montclair, NJ : Backbeat Books, 2016. | Includes index.
Identifiers: LCCN 2016000480 | ISBN 9781495049255 (pbk.)
Subjects: LCSH: Peiken, Shelly. | Lyricists--United States--Biography. |
  Popular music--Writing and publishing. | LCGFT: Biographies.
Classification: LCC ML423.P33 A3 2016 | DDC 782.42/164092--dc23
LC record available at http://lccn.loc.gov/2016000480

www.backbeatbooks.com

Contents

se·ri·al **adjective** \\'sir-ē-əl\\
The repetitive nature of similar acts performed
over a period of time.

Foreword

HANG AROUND THE music world awhile, and you'll often hear the phrase, "It all begins with a song." Hang around even longer, and you eventually realize *somebody* actually writes these songs. The incredibly talented Shelly Peiken has spent her life to date as part of a remarkable and ever-changing creative community of successful and professional songwriters whose work you know and love, even if you've never known her good name and excellent face. So if you've ever sat in your car or on a subway or around your backyard singing "Bitch" made famous by Meredith Brooks, or "What a Girl Wants" by Christina Aguilera, or dozens of other familiar songs sung by everyone from The Pretenders to Celine Dion to Keith Urban to Britney Spears, then it's definitely time you get properly introduced to the funny, smart and beautiful woman who did so much to bring those songs to life.

Confessions of a Serial Songwriter offers you the tremendous pleasure of really getting to know Shelly Peiken—and then some. This is more than a great book that takes us inside this fascinating world of working songwriters—it's even better than that. This is an insightful, honest, often funny, emotional look inside the good, the bad, the ugly and ultimately the transcendent aspects of trying to lead a creative life inside a competitive career that—like most of them—is full of highs and lows, ups and downs, art and commerce. And as you follow this pop culture pilgrim's progress inside the world of music, as well as film, television and life generally, you soon begin to realize that this time it's extremely personal—and that songwriters are the soul inside the music machine that never stops. A little bit Nora Ephron, a little bit Carole King and a whole lot of fun, *Confessions of a Serial Songwriter* is ultimately a book about life, as all the best ones really are."

—*David Wild* is a Contributing Editor for *Rolling Stone*, a two-time Emmy nominated television writer and *New York Times* best-selling author.

Introduction

I AM NOT Sheryl Crow. Though sometimes I wish I were. I love how she sings. I love how she plays guitar. (I love how she does it all in eight-inch strappy heels.) She writes songs that speak to my heart and other bodily parts. And, she seems like a really nice lady. But like I said, "I'm not Sheryl Crow." So who am I?

I am the young girl who was riding her bike around her Long Island neighborhood one summer day and passed a car with the window open and the radio on. The most amazing sound was heading right toward me—almost knocked me off my bike. It was Karen Carpenter singing "Close to You." It put a spell on me. All I wanted to do was follow that car and catch the magic.

I wrote my first song soon afterwards on a used piano in the den of my family's split-level home. My parents paid $19,000 for the house and $150 for the piano. Most pianos were shiny and lacquered. This one had a textured black and white "stucco" finish. It was the oddest-looking piano I'd ever seen. Nevertheless, I couldn't keep my hands off of it. My father gently informed me that the melody to this first song was similar, if not identical to, "Hatikvah," the Israeli national anthem. That was my first taste of copyright infringement. It was as if I had given up my virginity and something went terribly wrong. It didn't stop me. I began compiling lyrics in those composition books with the faux-marbled black and white cardboard covers that ironically matched that strange piano. My parents could see I needed guidance, so they hired a piano teacher, Mr. Milken. He tried to get me started with some classical pieces, but I wouldn't have any of it. I had caught sight of a stack of sheet music in his briefcase—popular songs like "What the World Needs Now Is Love," "I'll Be There" and…"Close to You." For God sakes, let me in! I convinced my mother to instruct Mr. Milken to bypass the classical and let me have my way with one pop song a week.

Fascinated with chord progressions and how moving from one particular triad to another could manipulate mood, I had no use for the melodic function of my right hand. Why bother playing the melody when I could just *sing* the melody while plunking out the accompanying chord changes with both hands?

Poor Mr. Milken. He had no purpose. I was in my own little world. One time I turned around and he was sleeping. I didn't care; I was just using him. He was my dealer. The drugs were in his briefcase.

In-between "lessons," I discovered I could extract the chord progression from my favorite song and write my own song on top of it. A single progression suggested an endless choice of melodies. It was like creating a drawing through tracing paper. I could *imitate* the emotional arc of a piece of music until I got the hang of its lines and curves… how it flowed from one section to another—*the tension and release*. Eventually, I could do it all by myself without the training wheels. The art of crafting a song was becoming second nature.

Carly Simon would become the soundtrack to my teenage years. Something about the way she expressed herself pulled me into her world and made me think about mine. I listened to her records *all* the time.

I listened to other records too: Carole King, Billy Joel, Joni Mitchell, James Taylor, Jackson Browne. They were all able to reach a place inside of me with their self-examination, honesty, incongruities, longings, and whimsical pleasures.

In college, my own musical ideas began echoing from that same place— the place where these artists started the fire. Only I was expressing *my* observations, *my* whimsical pleasures. I didn't know what I'd do with these ideas or if anyone would ever hear them or how I'd even get anyone to listen… but it didn't matter. They came and I received them. There wasn't a choice.

The lure of a piano was visceral. It was my happy place, even when I was miserable—*especially* when I was miserable. It was where I went when I needed to cope with life's uncertainties.

My songs were personal. I never considered anyone else would be interested in singing them. As far as I knew, whoever sang a song wrote the song they sang.

So after college, I headed for New York and formed a band thinking maybe I could get a record deal. I was pretty sure at that point I was meant to share my songs with the Universe, like Carly Simon. For whatever reason, the powers that "were" didn't agree. We'll never know if the powers were right about that. Who knows what might have happened if I'd persisted. Sometimes it can take years for an overnight success to succeed.

One thing's for sure: along with the privilege of making your own records comes the challenge of summoning an endless stream of inspired material and the pressure to stay at the top of your game—year after year. Terrifying. In hindsight, I don't know if I would have had the fortitude to promote myself, to tour, to show up, to prevail, and to withstand the scrutiny. Besides, I really liked coming home to Sushi, my cat. So…maybe the powers were right. At the risk of sounding like a songwriter, perhaps it wasn't meant to be.

But, I was a "SongJunkie." Writing them allowed me to expose emotions that were hard for me to express. If I couldn't make my own record, I had to find a different path that would keep them at the center of my life.

The Universe must have concurred, because after yet another gig at CBGB's (a Lower East Side rock club), with no offer to be the next Carly (or Carole or Joni), Hit & Run Music, a small boutique publishing company, invited me to be a songwriter on their roster. Joey Gmerek, their creative rep, had come to see me play. He said Hit & Run would help me get my songs to recording artists, keep me up-to-date on who was looking for material, arrange collaborations. I wondered if *this* could be the different path. I accepted their offer.

Soon, I was writing for pop stars that were vying for position on mainstream radio. Pop stars that *had* the x-factor, and were comfortable singing an "outside" song—a song written by a *serial* songwriter, just one who never got her own record deal. I also began writing *with* artists, because many of them enjoyed the adventure of collaboration and were not intimidated by someone who could take their ingredients (listen to their ideas) and help them bake their cake (write their song).

And that's what I've been doing since I signed that first publishing deal: writing songs for and with the artists who sing them. Totally self-contained bands that write their own material—I'm not on their radar—they don't need me. And that's okay; I'm having a very satisfying career—sometimes even exhilarating.

But it's been a bumpy ride. The music business has changed, more so lately, than ever. These are the stories of my journey—the ups, the downs, the in-betweens.

"Songwriters in the Round" at The Mint in L.A. with Kevin Griffin (Better Than Ezra).

The Muse

I WENT TO college at the University of Maryland. I chose Maryland not because of the "Textile and Human Apparel" program (which they offered) or the breathtaking campus (which it had) or the out-of-state government-assisted tuition (which I needed), but because when I visited the school "Cowgirl in the Sand" was wafting across fraternity row from an open window. I *loved* "Cowgirl in the Sand." That was that. Songs are powerful.

I majored in something called Fashion Merchandising. I know it doesn't have a particularly scholarly ring to it, but Maryland had a diverse curricula and I always thought it would be interesting to design, assemble, and put forth a line of clothing. It didn't occur to me to major in music. After all, music was my joy...my pleasure. Work was supposed to be work. I probably could have used a little more time to think about who I *really* wanted to be when I grew up. Where was the "gap year" in the 1970s?

I wound up boarding at a sorority house because it was the only on-campus housing available at the time. This particular sorority was populated by Southern debutante daughters of wealthy businessmen. They wore preppy rugby shirts, headbands and Docksiders. I wore overalls, bandanas and earth sandals—the token Jewish girl from middle class Long Island. They said, "Innit nice" and "*Warsh*ington DC." I said, "Why are you *tawking* like that?" I didn't really fit in. There was, however, a semi-tuned, wobbly, black matte baby grand in the living room of TriDelt and *that* was a blessing. At least there was a place to express myself on this strange turf, and there was much to tell. After all, your first semester of college wakes you up. That's when it occurs to you that you're more than just an extension of your parents or your hometown or your high school.

I liked my studies well enough. I was thrilled with my straight B-minuses. I enjoyed learning how to assess the bias of an A-line dress in a store window and recreate it on my Singer sewing machine. But by second semester, I desperately missed people who *tawked* like me, so I made plans to transfer to F.I.T. (Fashion Institute of Technology) in New York City, where I'd be around the corner from the Garment District and a hop-skip away from on-site training. But then I changed my mind, because a few weeks before the end of freshman year, I fell in love.

"Jake" was adorable, scruffy and sandy haired—exactly *not* my type... that would be adorable, scruffy and *dark* haired. The first time I saw him he was calling to my roommate, "Ginger," from the street outside our second floor window because he wanted to "have a look" at her homework. I should have known right then he was trouble. I shouted down, "Ginger's not here...I'll tell her you came by." And then he disappeared.

The next day I was sitting on the front steps and there he was again, skateboarding down College Avenue, cuter than the day before. I must have said something like, "Hey," and he said something like "Hey," and before I knew it I was on that skateboard with him. He laughed. I squealed, and in the next few minutes something happened that would affect me for the next, I'm embarrassed to say, thirty years. There was no turning back. My father ripped up the check for F.I.T.

Jake started coming around to see me. In my mind it was obvious we were crazy for each other. I'm still not sure what was going on in *his* mind. Rumor had it he had a girlfriend, but this was college. All bets were off. Statuses changed weekly.

I was sensible and cerebral; Jake was spontaneous and carefree. Perhaps I was attracted to qualities I secretly wanted to have. He bounced in and out of my life, little reprieves from his girlfriend I supposed. I lived for those elusive visits. If I couldn't have all of him, I would take what I could get.

There were nights we'd end up in his bed or in my bed kissing and pressing our bodies together. Years later, I would thank myself for not giving him the one thing I couldn't take back.

The musical floodgates opened. When my feelings are that alive and accessible, songs write themselves. I don't have to wait for inspiration. It oozes from every pore. After many hours behind my Singer, I'd escape to the fine arts building on the far side of campus and the sanctuary of a tiny practice room (furnished with an old but impeccably-tuned upright), where songs tumbled out of me. I didn't necessarily know what words would come out of my mouth, until my hands landed on the keys. And, I didn't necessarily know where my hands would land, until they touched down. It was spontaneous—discovery as opposed to contrivance. There were no guarantees. How was I going to get Jake to love me as much as I loved him? I never found the answer, but that was okay. It wasn't about the answer. It was about trying to *find* it.

Over summer break, I received only two handwritten letters from him. Remember those? And one phone call. Remember *those?* He was a cook in a crab house on the Maryland shore. I was a waitress three hundred miles north at a seafood restaurant on the waterfront in my hometown. My uniform was short. My pigtails were long. My legs were lean and toned and tan. I knew guys were thinking about me long after their lobster was gone. Why wasn't Jake? I held on to the delusional idea that when we returned for sophomore year, I'd officially be his girl. It was a summer of magical thinking.

I can't remember if he invited me or if I invited myself (I probably invited myself), but at the end of that endless summer, I drove my mother's station wagon to Jake's parents' home in New Jersey. Elton John and Kiki Dee's "Don't Go Breaking My Heart" was in steady rotation—on every station—I couldn't escape it.

He took me to the beach where he introduced me to banana coladas and did a convincing impression of someone who wanted to be there. Then we sat on a bench in the moonlight watching the waves crash on the rocks. I was wearing my blue and white sundress, the one that always made the impossible possible. This time my magic dress was powerless. He told me he was getting back together with *her.* I knew that probably meant he already had. I wanted to kiss him in spite of the horrible news—one last desperate attempt to get him to love me back.

I was in no shape to be behind a wheel so I stayed the night. The fantasy I had had driving down in the car, of him telling me how much he had missed me, kissing and pressing our bodies together, was shattered. He was in the next room, sleeping like a baby, unburdened for having told me the truth, his conscience clear. In the morning I drove home. "Don't Go Breaking My Heart" on every station. Have they no mercy?

The first day back at school, Jake was at my door dangling that carrot as if nothing had happened. But something *did* happen and I couldn't deny it any more. I stopped seeing him. I dated other guys, even had some meaningful relationships, but he was always there peripherally in a corner of my heart.

I can't tell you how many songs I've written over the years that were inspired by that one *relationship-in-my-mind*. It's good for any songwriter to have a muse, especially a muse that breaks your heart. Because if there isn't something in the present beckoning you to write about it, you can close your eyes and summon how you felt in the past. Imagining and remembering all over again: the euphoria of what could have been and the disappointment of what never was. There is always another song.

SongSex

...IS THE ACT of getting together with someone and writing a song. Good "SongSex" is when an idea effortlessly unfolds and you don't have to ask yourself if it's good, because you know it is. And, you don't necessarily need a cigarette afterwards (unless you smoke), but you *do* get a "SongHigh" from it. You just want to listen to it; then listen to it again, and again. You want to play it for your best friend as soon as possible.

The barometer for good *SongSex* can be measured by how satisfying the experience is, whether or not you get off and if you are still basking in its glow in the morning. You feel like an itch has been scratched...like you don't have to write another song for a few days. You've been sated.

However, sometimes you might have bad *SongSex*. When this occurs, it's *awkward*. You usually don't call your partner the next day. If you do, you lie...not just because you don't want to hurt his (or her) feelings or make him feel like he wasted your time (or like you wasted his), but mostly because you're embarrassed that you had anything to do with it.

Now, bad *SongSex* is not so bad if you have it with people in your comfort zone...people who realize good *SongSex* is part luck and they still love you and don't think it's entirely your fault if you don't collectively reach a climax. There is no finger-pointing or blame-placing. They are people you can laugh with someday about that unfortunate mistake you wrote...and called a song.

Snapshot: Crystal Blue Persuasion

It's 1969. That's right. I was there. "Crystal Blue Persuasion" is coming from the transistor radio. My father is flipping burgers on the freestanding charcoal grill wearing plaid swim trunks, a shirt that doesn't match and rubber sandals. There's no place else he'd rather be. My Mom, in horn-rimmed sunglasses and culottes, is coming out of the sliding door with the coleslaw and pickles. They are in their heyday. Paying a mortgage, going to drive-ins; still in love. A Buick and a Rambler in the driveway out front. My cousins and I are doing cartwheels on the lawn—even the boys.

I'm not sure what a "Crystal Blue Persuasion" is but whatever it is makes me feel like everything will be okay, especially the modulation. The sun is shining. My parents are alive. Life is as simple as it will ever be.

(Clockwise) My Dad, Mom, sister Marla and me.

Movin' on Up

COLLEGE WASN'T HOW I imagined it would be when I first heard "Cowgirl in the Sand" wafting from that window (the version in my head was more *Woodstock* in spirit—less organized). Sorority life involved rushing, pledging, mandatory Monday night meetings, spring formals, and secret handshakes. I didn't have the impetus, however, to start over when campus housing became available. So I stayed put. And like a chameleon, I learned to blend in. I even formed some quality friendships with a few of the Southern debutante daughters.

After graduating, I returned to Long Island and moved back in with my parents; same small bedroom I left when I was eighteen: orange shag rug, flowery wallpaper, and that fluorescent poster with its psychedelic message about war, children and "other living things." The lyrics to The Beach Boys' song "In My Room" were still taped to the outside of my door. It was odd to be back. Surrounded by the familiarity of those four walls, it was almost as if nothing had changed. Of course, so much had, and I knew I needed to move on.

So I found myself a tiny studio apartment in Forest Hills for $236 a month. (My father, the extremely frugal accountant, advised me that without a job on the horizon and only $500 in the bank, committing to a higher monthly nut would be irresponsible.) My Grandmother had given me a previously-owned walnut spinet piano as a college graduation gift;

In my room.

that, a bed and a toothbrush got me started. The apartment wouldn't fit much more. Seriously.

I interviewed for a couple of jobs on "Fashion (7th) Avenue" in New York City's Garment District, but I had an unsettling feeling I didn't belong there. Maybe my interest in fashion had more to do with the grace of a garment than the business of buying and selling it. This wasn't the first time I would question my personal GPS and it wouldn't be the last.

Still, I needed to pay my bills, and while combing through the want ads in the *New York Times*, I happened upon a blurb for a songwriting workshop that convened every Tuesday night at Uncle Lulu's on West 56th Street. It sounded like AA for songwriters; I couldn't wait to check it out.

There, in a windowless room at the back of that bar, is where I found my *people*. For so many years I had these symptoms…this condition…and I didn't know anyone else who had it. It turned out there *were* others, and now they were right in front of me—fellow song-a-holics. Over burgers and beer we listened and shared—"Songwriters Anonymous," except for the beer.

We observed each other's styles and techniques. Analyzed phrasing that resonated.

I like his key change on the bridge, her rhyme scheme, that AABA structure, that diminished chord; I've never used one. Oooh, I wanna try that.

Being a part of what was going on in that room every week was invaluable. It was a safe place to experiment and expand my palate.

I met boisterous and wild-haired Jesse there. He took notice of me as soon as I entered the room and didn't waste any time making his way over to my table, as if he knew we were destined to share some future path. (He would give this book its title many years later.) In the weeks that followed, Jesse took my hand and taught me how to navigate the subway system. He introduced me to Bleecker Street in Greenwich Village where the spirits of Dylan and Joni and James were alive and well. *"Why did it take me so long to find this?"* Aside from a couple of elementary school class trips to museums and the occasional Broadway musical with my family, The Big Apple had been uncharted territory. That was all about to change.

I took my newly polished songs and played my heart out wherever they'd let me—for free, of course. At the Bitter End, at Kenny's Castaways, I would have paid *them* if they had asked me. All this playing for free, however, was not paying the rent. So I had another look at the classifieds and saw that a brand new Hyatt Hotel was opening in midtown. In addition to the hundreds of positions for janitors, maids, concierge and bellman that needed to be filled, they would be hiring thirteen young women to serve cocktails in the chic, glass-enclosed structure that was suspended over the street below—The SunGarden.

Gasp. I'm a young woman; I can serve cocktails. In fact, I'm an excellent waitress. I'm friendly, I'm pretty, I have experience. I'll make a helluva lot more money than I can on 7th Avenue, and I'll have so much more time to write songs.

THE LINE OF applicants went on for blocks. This did not deter me. After an interview, a drug test and a lie detector test (apparently a lot of unscrupulous behavior went on in employee locker rooms), I got the job. I knew I would. I said good-bye to Calvin Klein and hello to Johnny Walker on the rocks. I was a little wary of telling my parents about this change of plan. It wouldn't be until many years later, when I became a parent myself, that I understood what they meant when they said, "We just want you to be happy."

The city was full of energy, light, chaos, talent, challenge, opportunity, lust, risk, danger, romance, color, and points of view. It fed my head; I was motivated, adrenalized, engaged. I couldn't imagine being anywhere else in the world. From waitressing tips alone, I was able to move from Queens into Manhattan. My first place was a $400 a month, cockroach-infested, 18'x10' dump on the ground floor of the only un-renovated brownstone on West 85th Street. I used the oven as a heat source and shared the shower with the water bugs. I didn't care. I put that shiny brown spinet up against the front window, which separated the apartment from the sidewalk, and serenaded the homeless man who slept outside against the trashcans. Sometimes I'd even take his requests.

N.Y.C. Apt. #1 ground floor…Columbus and 85th Street. When I last checked it was still the only un-renovated brownstone on the block.

After nine months in that shit hole, I made a friend while strolling Columbus Avenue—a friend whose father happened to own a building in the heart of the Village. There was a studio with an alcove available on the third floor. Elevator. Doorman. You just never know what can happen when you take a walk, especially in New York.

When I first laid my eyes on the empty unit, I was overcome by its vacancy…a vacancy for me to fill. The freshly painted white walls—a blank

View from third floor, N.Y.C., Apt #2, 12th Street and Broadway, garbage truck adjacent. ("Happy Bday Shellerina" spray-painted by my songwriter friend Jim Dyke on the building across the street.)

canvas of possibility. It was not without its drawbacks, though. Outside, the trash pick up area was just below the window near my bed and every morning at 1:00am, I'd be startled awake from the screech of the trucks and the shattering of glass bottles. Again, I didn't care; I was safe and above ground. No armies of cockroaches crawling out of holes in the walls. It was all uphill from there. I rode my ten-speed up and down Broadway, headphones affixed to my ears, "Who Can It Be Now?" It was definitely me!

As it turned out, aspiring songwriters were all over the city. I met Alex ("Don't Rush Me") Forbes at another workshop, The Songwriter's Circle. She seemed as obsessed as I was. We glommed onto each other and formed a little duo, Alex with her Guild D35 acoustic strapped across her back and me with a Casio keyboard perched atop a four-foot metal pole. The Casio had a convenient built-in drum-fill button, which I implemented without shame. Our performances were far from polished, but plenty of friends, family and fans showed up. Enthusiasm is contagious.

Alex and I started our own workshop, which we anointed "SongParty." This was long before you could put *the word* out on Facebook, but somehow *the word* spread anyway. In the course of a few months, *SongParty* grew

Shelly with Alexandra Forbes

to fifty fanatics who all craved the same three-minute fix. Every Monday night we checked our egos at the door and crammed into Alex's fifth floor walk-up with a bag of chips or a bottle of something in hand. We'd strum a guitar or play a home recording on a ghetto blaster. Knowing we had a room full of SongJunkies as an audience kept us eager to come up with a new work-in-progress every week...hungry for a critique...knowing it would make us better.

Word had it that record labels solicited material from independent song-writers. Why couldn't it be from one of us, maybe something for Sheena Easton, Cheap Trick, Oleta Adams or Laura Branigan? I recorded demos on a borrowed 4-track, reel-to-reel TEAC tape recorder, straddling the bathtub behind the shower curtain in order to get echo on my vocals. You did what you had to do with what you could afford.

Soon, I "graduated" from the Hyatt's SunGarden to the more upscale Trumpets Lounge where, instead of waitressing, I sang and played the shiny black Steinway. This promotion could very well have had something to do with the fact that I was dating (and doing some other things with) the hotel's assistant manager, but I like to think it was also because I had a little *qu'est-ce que c'est…je ne sais quoi.* I crooned away…"I Only Have Eyes for You," "Where or When," "Chances Are" and yes, the mandatory, "Feelings." Determined to set my repertoire apart from typical piano bar fare, I included the more contemporary "Deacon Blues," "Mary's Prayer," "Rhiannon" and of course Carly's greatest hits, "Legend," "Anticipation," and "You're So Vain." My thrift shop, vintage party dresses, blood-red lipstick and retro styled hair were good distractions from the obvious fact that I wasn't a stellar musician.

Taking nothing for granted, I did some inquiring and found Mike Longo, an accomplished jazz pianist who played with the likes of Dizzy Gillespie. I appealed to him for a crash course in piano bar shortcuts— tricks, segues, alternate chord inversions, smooth transitions from one song to another—whatever would get me through a shift with grace and a bit more sophistication. Mike was gracious and showed me what I'd need to get by.

There's no denying that this repeated practice and exposure, night after night, to more challenging material, made me more fluent and musically flexible. I was navigating new territory with ease. One's musical education comes from a blend of formal study *and* from taking advantage of the opportunities that come along while you're just living your life. I saw an opening and I went for it. And, I made sure I developed the skills to pull it off.

There was great pride in knowing I was officially making a living in the music business. The express train took me from Union Square to Grand Central at 4:30pm. After my set, it dropped me back off in the Village at 8:30pm. The three-hour workday allowed me plenty of time to write dozens of inconsequential songs. They were all rehearsals for the future. In-between them I lazed about, flipping through the pages of *Billboard,* dissecting the Hot 100. Who was this D. Warren? D. Child? H. Knight? (The names repeatedly listed as writers next to the biggest hits.) Would I ever see an "S. Peiken" next to a song on that chart—preferably toward the top?

One morning while having breakfast at a diner on 12th and University, I noticed a cute guy staring at me from the next booth. He said he remembered me from a Psych. 101 class, freshman year at Maryland. Impressive—that lecture had 700 students in it. Russell was funny, *really* funny. He asked for my number and as I opened the door to my apartment upon returning from breakfast the phone was already ringing. I broke up with the assistant manager.

By this time I was well into my twenties. My friends were starting to pair off and some of them were looking for someone just like Russell. But me? I didn't feel an immediate urge to merge. What was the rush? Time wasn't going anywhere; I had plenty of it. There were things I needed to do before I merged.

Then again, Russell and I *did* have a blast together. I was a corseted Apollonia to his Prince on Halloween night—we karaoke'd our way through "Purple Rain" on stage at Heartbreak (a 1980s West Village must-go-to dancehall). He whisked me off on jaunts to Jamaica, bought me silk bathrobes and crystal earrings, breakfasts, lunches and dinners, and great seats for Springsteen. I loved his family. Plus, like I said, he *was* really cute, and funny. *And* he was crazy about me, although I was pretty sure he was crazy about another girl or two also, but I ignored my suspicions: Laughter + travel + gifts + cute is a potent combination.

On occasion I'd look up at the crowd in-between songs at the piano bar and see Russell there, smiling proudly. I knew he was hoping that if we got married, and moved out to Long Island (where he grew up as well), a beautiful house would distract me from my ambition, and, a beautiful baby (or two) wouldn't hurt. What he didn't realize was that I was never going to be able to snuff out that fire. And…according to the latest edition of *Our Bodies, Ourselves*, I could safely delay starting a family for another ten years. And…I wasn't any less in love with New York City than when I had found her. But I loved him too. If I moved out of the city, it didn't mean I couldn't spend time *in* the city. Maybe, just maybe, I could have both. I wanted to try. So I walked down the aisle despite the whisper of doubt in my heart, and back to Long Island I went.

Then, after writing dozens more of those inconsequential songs, and getting "no thank yous" after countless submissions, I wrote one of consequence. Ironically, this happened one afternoon while I was sitting at the ivory baby grand Russell bought me when we moved into that beautiful house in East Rockaway. I was home alone that day (as I often am when I manage to catch lightning in a bottle). No one was listening or sitting in the next room judging silently. There was no other opinion I was obliged to consider. (I have come to cherish collaboration, but sometimes having *SongSex* all by myself is divine. Like masturbation, I know just how I like it.)

I stared at the keys. They were my friends. I closed my eyes. My hands settled on a straightforward G chord. *What's on your mind, girl?* I saw Jake standing on the lawn outside the sorority house—my trusted muse.

I hear you calling from the street outside my window,

And then…something with a bit more tension and irony to balance out the simplicity of the first line:

You keep returning just to tell me that you're gone.

I'm not saying this was a conscious strategy. It doesn't work like that. I try not to overthink…I let subconscious thoughts find their way to my lips. Those are the ones that matter, because they never lie.

Jake couldn't live with me, but he couldn't live without me. He needed me; he just didn't know it. And so the chorus:

You carry your heart.
No one can hold
All of that weight on your shoulders.
You carry your heart.
And when it gets cold you run to me.
See…you can't carry your heart alone.

That last line crystallized the concept: *When will you realize that you need me?* I didn't know it was crystallized at the time, but it's clear to me now.

For $300, musician Steve Skinner created a demo with his MIDI keyboard and a Linn 9000 drum machine. I paid Nikki Gregoroff $150 to sing and I was good to go.

Producer Ric Wake was making a record with a ballsy and soulful singer, Leslie Wunderman aka Taylor Dayne. A couple of fellow songwriters, whose material was already being considered for her record, suggested I submit something to Ric as well. (This was back in the day when there was an abundance of opportunity and competitors shared information freely.) So I wrote a song with my friend "Dan." I didn't actually care for it all that much but it seemed compatible with the rest of Taylor's material. I put it on a cassette tape and, for good measure, I added one more song—the inspired "Carry Your Heart."

There's something to be said for bypassing gatekeepers and getting your demo directly to the artist if you can. Nothing compares with the power a song can have if it has the chance to beeline straight into somebody's heart. It just so happened that Taylor lived very near my beautiful house and one night, I mustered the nerve to drive over to *her* beautiful house to deliver my song(s). My colleague, Jeff Franzel, who has an impressive memory, recalls my account of the event like this: Taylor answered the door and I said, "Wow, I thought you were black." This was pre-YouTube when it was unlikely you'd know what an artist looked like before their debut album was released. I had only heard her voice on a demo or two and it was unusual for a white girl to sing with so much soul. So maybe I *did* say that and have conveniently chosen to forget it, because, come on…wouldn't you want to forget saying something so clumsy? What *I* remember is leaving the cassette under her doormat, getting into my car and making a mad dash back to my beautiful house, but Jeff *could* be right.

Ric Wake called the next day. Taylor loved it—the second song. The first one—the one I wrote with Dan? Not so much. *Uh oh…what to tell Dan?* But you can't control this stuff. So I said, "That's fantastic! When will she cut it?"

With Clive Davis's nod (the president of Arista—Taylor's label), "Carry Your Heart" was the first song of mine to be professionally recorded, and like I would for many others down the line, I listened to the final mastered recording over and over. I had written it by myself, every word, every note. It was inspired by something true. Not something conjured, and someone loved it enough to sing it. Someone validated me. In my mind, I was Sally Field accepting the Oscar for *Places in the Heart. Taylor liked it. She really liked it!* I was finally and officially a professional songwriter and I'd be lying if I said that that didn't give me a kind of courage I didn't have the day before.

As for my marriage to Russell, it never took off. We couldn't laugh hard enough. His foot was on the accelerator—I was still highlighting those passages in *Our Bodies, Ourselves*. I guess I couldn't blame him completely if he looked "elsewhere" to make up for the 100% I couldn't give. So I took my newfound courage and on a rainy New Year's Day, while he was lying on the couch in that state between sleep and lucidity, football droning in the background, I gave him a kiss, put my cat Sushi in her carrier and left our beautiful house.

He did not object. I would ask for three months rent and the use of the car until I got back on my feet. I didn't want anything else. My freedom was a painful enough exchange. I drove toward the city in a deluge with my eyes full of tears and a windshield full of rain, unable to distinguish one from the other. It was all a blur. Bruce was singing "One step up, two steps back," but honestly, it felt like the other way around.

My 12th Street landlord took me back. I moved into Apt 8L, a slightly higher, larger unit with a separate bedroom, 3 closets, a dishwasher, and a clear view of the famous Strand Book Store below.

Carly Simon

ON A BEAUTIFUL spring afternoon in New York City, I stepped into an elevator in a building on West 57th Street and there she was—Carly Simon. The one who made me ponder "Anticipation"…the loveliness of the time spent in the moments we await something we desire. The one who must have been trying to tell me something when she sang:

> *But you say it's time we moved in together*
> *And raised a family of our own, you and me.*
> *Well, that's the way I've always heard it should be,*
> *You want to marry me, we'll marry.*

Having just walked out on a failed marriage, I finally understood the irony in that song.

The doors closed and it was just the two of us, and the air in-between. My heart was pounding out of my chest. I had maybe twenty seconds to either say something to Carly Simon or forever regret *not* saying something. Or say something and forever regret *saying* it. What if I opened my mouth and nothing came out? What if something came out and it was strange?

All of a sudden, there was nothing to decide because Carly Simon said to *me*, "Don't I know you from somewhere?"

WHAT? What I wanted to say was: *Are you kidding me? You don't understand…I slept with your albums under my pillow. I am me because of you. I love you Carly Simon.*

What I said, however, was, "Nope, I don't think so."

She replied calmly, "Are you sure? You look so familiar."

And what I thought was: *Of course I look familiar. I know you so well; it only makes sense that you know me too.*

What I said was, "Oh yes, I'm quite sure."

I have no regrets. What I had to say to her could not be summed up in a twenty second ride to the 26th floor. I would have had to leave too much out, and it all mattered. No one could be that brief. I told myself that she "knew." She must have seen something in the obvious way I tried *not* to stare or felt something in that air in-between us. I told myself, "one day I will have another chance." So far I haven't, but there's still time.

So Sue Me

WHEN "CARRY YOUR Heart" was released on Taylor Dayne's debut album in 1987, *Billboard* reviewed it as one of the songs to watch. (If I'd saved the magazine I could tell you exactly what it said, but trust me it was quite favorable.) When I saw it in black and white, I had one of those moments when you wonder how you could ever have doubted your destiny. It was all meant to be. It just took its sweet time, but now my path to fame and fortune was clear. After all, my reasoning went, record labels revered *Billboard* and therefore, when the suits at Arista saw that review they would have no choice but to release the song as a single.[1]

Not long after my destiny had been secured, I was boarding a plane and heard elevator-style music coming through American Airlines' tinny overhead speakers. Something sounded very familiar.

OMG…it's "Carry Your Heart." This is big. They already have an instrumental version. Arista didn't waste any time. It's going be a single for sure! On my very first recording no less!

---

[1] There is considerably more income from a single than from a song that simply exists on an album: potentially hundreds of thousands of dollars in airplay or "performance royalties," paid to the writers by their PRO (Performing Rights Organization such as ASCAP, BMI, SESAC). On top of that, there are TV and film usages, sheet music, T-shirts, video games, key chains, toys—the list goes on. Aside from the financial windfall, there is a great deal more prestige attached to a single. Songwriters *want* singles.

I was traveling alone and had no one with whom to share this fantastic news. However, as the song progressed, it took a different turn.

Wow, you know what? Now it sounds a lot like…Umm…that song from Tootsie…Umm… "It Might Be You." Then I realized, it *was* "It Might Be You." *OMG…I think I ripped off "It Might Be You."*

I checked the playlist in the in-flight magazine just to be sure. Yup… *Tootsie.* I thought I was going to puke and we hadn't even taken off yet. I *loved* that song from *Tootsie*, so much so that I inadvertently rewrote it with different lyrics. It must have been lodged somewhere in a crevice of my auditory memory.

I was finally going to have a *big fat hit* and Stephen Bishop, someone I greatly admired, was going to sue me. And that would surely tarnish my reputation before I even got out of the gate, wreak havoc on my psyche, my career, cost me a publishing deal! It was the only time in my life I was hoping my song would *not* be a single. I sat there frozen, staring bug-eyed at the barf bag in the pocket of the seat in front of me for the remainder of the flight.

As luck would have it, Arista was not *Billboard*'s bitch. "Carry Your Heart" wasn't released as a radio single, so it was very unlikely I would be sued for a song that didn't make a ton of money, because usually a piece of much less than a small fortune would not be worth the effort (or the legal fees). I let go a sigh of relief. Careful what you wish for.

P.S. When "Carry Your Heart" was reviewed in Billboard, *I shared my excitement with my friend, Evan Lamberg, who was an intern at Jobete Music at the time. (He has since gone on to become a major player in the music publishing industry.) He told me he knew a songwriter who, after his first recording, waited eleven years for his first single. I thought, "That's not going to happen to me. I'll die before I can wait that long." My first U.S. single, would be released eleven years later.*

With my Dad, Leon Peiken, circa 1980.

Underneath It All

I WAS MAD at my father. He made rules I wanted to break and drew boundaries I wanted to cross. I loved him. I hated him. That's how it is when you're fifteen. One day we had a big fight and as he stood in the hallway outside my bedroom trying to reason with my raging hormones, I threw a hairbrush at him and screamed, "I hate you—get out of my life!" And then I slammed the door in his face.

We didn't talk...or at least, I not to him, for what seemed like a year... in retrospect it might only have been a few months. Either way, it was long enough. I resisted all temptation to respond to any question he asked me or to participate in any conversation he initiated. How this must have hurt him.

One night as I walked past the kitchen where my father was sitting at the table in his robe and slippers doing someone's taxes, he said something to me, like he did every night hoping to end the cold war. I can't remember what it was, but it didn't matter. Like I said, I ignored him. As he shook his head I heard him mutter, "Bitch, bitch, bitch." I knew he loved me—more than life itself, and it seemed harsh. But I was definitely acting like a bitch; I deserved to be called one, even by my father. It might have stuck with me unconsciously.

The Mother App

I AM PRETTY certain a Mother App was not included on my operating system when I was born. Thus, I was never absolutely sure I wanted to be a parent. So what? Don't *all* women have their doubts?

The answer is—"no." I have friends who always knew—they *wanted* children. Full Stop. End of story. As for me, although my biological clock was ticking, ticking, ticking, it was really my psychological clock I was having trouble with.

Delaying the decision was like hitting the snooze button on an alarm clock. Every two years or so, I would smack it and buy myself some more time.

Here were some of my concerns:

1. If I had a baby, I'd have to grow up.

2. If I grew up, I'd be closer to my death.

3. Pregnancy leads to stretch marks and saggy boobs.

4. I'd be kowtowing to cultural expectations as well as pressure from my mother, sister, and girlfriend Lucy.

5. I'd gain weight.

6. I would no longer be on call for the ebb and flow of creative musings.

7. What if I left my baby at the mall?

8. I'd lose my edge and start writing lullabies.

9. I'd have to give up my Miata. (See next chapter)

10. Having that much more to love means having that much more to lose.

Snapshot: I Saw the Light

I'm fifteen and I've broken up with "Andy." I know I've made a huge mistake and I absolutely *must* get him back…especially because I heard through the grapevine he might ask out "Karen What's-Her-Name." So I write the words to "I Saw the Light" on really pretty stationery…"and I ran out before…but I won't do it any more." I am certain *this song* can save our love. I give it a spritz of Shalimar and send it to him in the mail. He takes me back, but then I break up with him again.

The Antidote

ALEX *(SONGPARTY)* FORBES and I had a theory back when we were palling around New York City after my divorce from Russell: *Every new relationship is the antidote for the one that came before it.* For instance, if you were with a workaholic who didn't pay enough attention to you, next time you might be drawn to a drifter who had time on his hands. Or if you were with a Wall Street banker whose mind was on money, you might gravitate toward a painter whose mind was on art. Or if you were with someone you suspected was unfaithful…whatever wasn't working…you had an opportunity to find someone who could perhaps heal you—*if* they were the opposite of what hurt you.

Makes sense, right? Why would you speed head-on toward the same collision twice? Why not aim for a different one? Change is good. Or better yet, if possible, have no collision at all.

I met Adam at a jingle session in New York in 1990. I'm a little ashamed to say (but obviously not ashamed enough) that it was during a SAG strike. While hard-working jingle singers were walking the picket lines trying to improve their contracts, I was a "scab"—a temporary replacement. I learned very quickly how to put the sexy in peanut butter and the pep in Dr. Pepper. Adam and his Dad, Al Gorgoni, had written a jingle for Kool-Aid, and, on the recommendation of a mutual friend, they called me to sing it.

Adam, 1991.

Adam was adorable and scruffy and *dark*. My type! His eyes were big and colorful and intense. When he smiled, it eased the burden on his face, like the sun breaking through the clouds. I would learn later he was just coming off of a relationship himself. She was apparently even more intense than he was. With my Alannah Myles-style hair, black leather jeans, and blue tinted contact lenses, I may have been too rock-star-in-my-own-mind for him at the time. I told him I had a band and wanted to put him on my mailing list…could I have his address? He gave it to me and I invited him to my gigs, but he never came. I didn't even hear from him after that. It was a shame too, because he lived on East 11th Street and I lived on East 12th. How convenient it would have been to frolic with him in a city like New York. How fun to shine my sun on his cloud.

Unbeknownst to me, shortly after that, Adam moved to Los Angeles to pursue a career in music for film and TV. I frolicked instead with Alex and Jesse. New York City was our playground.

Meanwhile, Taylor Dayne's album wound up selling 3 million copies. This meant that even though "Carry Your Heart" wasn't a single, Arista would pay me about $200,000, based on the statutory mechanical rate at

Alannah Myles–style hair/blue contacts.

the time. Soon after that, I signed my first co-publishing agreement with Hit & Run Music for which I received a reasonable advance. And, soon after *that*, I was seduced by a television commercial that showed a spiffy little vehicle winding through country roads under starry skies with the whimsical instrumental "Sleep Walk" crooning in the background. I *loved* "Sleep Walk." Plus, I had a lot more than $500 to my name, so I bought myself that car—a shiny white Miata—and then I quit my "day job" at the piano bar.

My new two-seater convertible was a symbol of perseverance and freedom. I would no longer be left behind on summer weekends while everybody else was taking off for their timeshare on Fire Island. My friend Jamie and I got our *own* timeshare on Fire Island and we had a car to get us to the ferry in style. On Friday afternoons we'd hightail up the Long Island Expressway to Bay Shore…"Brown skin shining in the sun," "Top pulled down," "Wayfarers on"—two very happy girls driving around in a Don Henley song.

Whatever causes youth to be so bold, we had it. One Sunday night, we defied the warnings to stay put during an approaching hurricane and instead

With Jamie Marcus; Fire Island bound.

caught the last ferry off the island. They weren't kidding about the hurricane. Through thunder, lightning and pouring rain, we white-knuckled it all the way back to the city under the precarious shelter of a vinyl roof. And then we laughed about it for days.

I was having such a good time persevering and being free, I forgot about Adam—for about a year that is. Just around twelve months later, I was in Los Angeles and went to a party in a house nestled in Laurel Canyon hosted by songwriter Anne ("Torn") Preven. It just so happened Adam had gone to college with Anne and he was at the party too. He made his way over to me without realizing who I was. I had toned down my look by then. When I told him my name he said, "Oh, I know you…you sang a jingle for me and my Dad." I thought he was making it up. It sounded like a pick-up line… even though I *had* sung a jingle or two, or three. I said something like, "Oh, yeah? What was the product?"

"I think it was Kool Aid," he answered. *Omagod…it's that guy.* Suddenly there was nobody else in the room but us, or if there was, they were invisible. We talked for hours. You know how they say you just know? I knew—he was *the* one. Plus, we found each other twice. It surely felt like the Universe was trying to get us together and this time Adam was ready.

Adam definitely fell into *antidote* territory. First of all Russell, my ex, was exactly my height. Once when we were dating, he came to pick me up in roller skates. I guess he wanted to see what it would feel like if I were shorter than him. But with Adam being six foot one, I could bend my head back when we kissed, even when I was wearing heels.

Also, Russell was carefree and silly. Perhaps, in marrying him, I finally got my taste of what it would have been like to be in a relationship with Jake. What I really needed was someone steadfast—devoted. And, Adam *was* funny; he just had a drier sense of humor. Plus, he was solid; he was there for me. The biggest opposite of all—Russell wanted the music to go away; Adam was writing his own. We understood each other's addiction. We were under the spell of the same drug. I didn't have to explain or convince or feel guilty.

The problem was, I lived in New York and he lived in Los Angeles, which made things a little tricky, *and* expensive. We couldn't be in touch 24/7 like you can today. Our monthly landline phone bills were hundreds of dollars. Still, we managed never to spend more than six weeks apart. I'd pick him up at Newark Airport in the middle of a snowstorm, we'd bungee his road case into my tiny trunk and fishtail our way back to the city through the Holland Tunnel. Or, I'd go to Los Angeles and rent a convertible and soar through the canyons after dark, night-blooming jasmine in the air, thinking, *"I could get used to this."*

When things looked like they were working out, Adam encouraged me to make the move west. Indeed, there was plenty of music business to be had out there. In the back of my mind I knew time *was* moving forward, and, like I said, I knew he was *the* one.

But who's kidding who? The idea had a familiar ring to it. It reminded me of Russell luring me out to Long Island against my better judgment, and we all know how that turned out. *That* time I could bounce right back to the city when it was over. What if that happened again?

I hung onto New York for dear life, not sure I could survive outside of it, no matter who I loved in California. Adam learned how to play "Sleep

Walk" on his guitar and serenaded me (or my answering machine) nightly. It was romantic and clever; I still wouldn't budge.

There was another reason I was apprehensive about leaving the East Coast. My mother had been diagnosed with Parkinson's disease a few years earlier. It was in its beginning stages but we knew what was to come. Slowly but surely, her nervous system would take her hostage. My dad was an excellent observer of her fluctuating symptoms and adjusted her daily cocktail of meds accordingly. With his watchful eye, her condition was progressing slower than it might have otherwise. Still, this made it harder to leave.

I had been visiting with my parents one night, and on the way back into the city while driving over the 59th Street Bridge I took in the Manhattan skyline like never before…the twinkling of a million lights coming from a million windows. I thought about all the people who were sitting down to dinner, coming home from work, going to work, making love, breaking up, living their New York City lives. I had always wanted to be a part of it, and now I was. I was a small but significant piece of its mosaic. I thought about all the margaritas I served just to get out of Queens. How I finally wrote a song that made it possible to quit serving those margaritas. All the rejection I had endured. And now one of those lights was mine. My modest apartment marked my territory. The keys to its door were dangling from the ignition. My name was on a mailbox. No one could kick me out. Or ask me to leave. No one.

Adam and I had been in a relationship for two years at that point. He suggested that I was self-involved…that my life was all about *my* life, *my* career, *my* independence, *my* Miata. And speaking of my Miata…he had this theory that there was a reason why I was drawn to such a small vehicle: There was just enough room for *me*.

That's not fair, I would argue. There *is* a passenger seat. There *is* room for someone else. Besides, I was *trying* to expand. I really was. In fact, I had this recurring dream of driving to the airport in my Miata trying desperately to get to Los Angeles. At the end of that dream there's no room for the car on the plane. I had another recurring dream in which I was flying across the country *in* my Miata. I didn't need the stupid plane. But truth be told, in my dreams, no one *was* ever in the passenger seat. I *was* alone; Adam had a point.

So in 1994, after much soul searching and blessings from my parents, I did it. I made the transplant. I left my beloved N.Y. My mom was in the best hands she could be in. I loved Adam and I believed I'd found my *antidote*. Still, it was not without a heavy heart. I remained madly in love with the city that dared me to discover myself—the city where my GPS finally kicked in. It's hard to move on when you feel like you haven't had enough. (It's hard for me to imagine ever getting enough of N.Y.) Furthermore, this wasn't just a move downtown. This was a new coast, new friends, new culture, new weather, brand spankin' new life. There would be a much greater distance over which to bounce back if things didn't work out, but I was hopeful they would. Regardless, I couldn't look over my shoulder at my empty apartment before I closed the door—a blank canvas of possibility again…for somebody else.

Sushi was with me as she was when I moved in with Russell. But I knew we were headed for a healthier situation this time. (She'd even have a friend—Adam's cat, James.) As much as I loved N.Y., I *wanted* to be able to love L.A. and to prove to my recurring dreams that I could fill that passenger seat.

My Miata was on its way to L.A. too, via flatbed. We would gleefully reunite two weeks later in a parking lot in Encino. I can't say Sushi and James became fast friends. He was into her. She—him? Not so much. Oh well, they would deal.

A few weeks after Sushi and I started to get our feet (and paws) firmly planted in California, my sister called. My Dad's aorta had ruptured. Back east I flew…staring at the tray table in front of me for five straight hours, not knowing if, when I landed, he'd be alive. He was, but he died the next day. My Daddy…the one who dodged the hairbrush…the one who called me a "bitch." The one I found with his head in his hands weeping on the corner of Columbus and 85th Street after he saw the holes in the walls of the apartment I was so excited about moving into. I loved him so. My poor Daddy, my hero. After all the times he had saved me, there was absolutely nothing I could do to save him.

There was a second stage to this devastatingly new reality. My Mom, suddenly abandoned by her life partner and soul mate…who would care for her? My sister would be close by, but *I* had relocated. I could call her daily. Interrupt her grief with ten-minute chats. *You okay Mom? I know. I miss him too. Are you taking your pills?* As if that would put a dent in her loneliness, or her decline, or my guilt.

When I returned to L.A., I slowly and solemnly resumed my life. What choice do we have? Adam was the bearer of my sadness. He kept me busy doing some jingles with him. I could be Beach Blanket Barbie as long as he was my Ken. We knew the jingle life was temporary…a steppingstone to a film for him and a hit song for me. I made friends. Found new collaborators. Adam cheered on every song that was recorded, no matter how trivial. My father would have been happy to know that I was content in my new home and with my new man. I was a little surprised myself.

Adam was the "alternative" in my otherwise mainstream world. He turned me on to NPR and Talk Radio. I kept track of our frequent flyer miles; he booked the tickets. I navigated; he drove. I cooked dinner; he took out the trash and scooped the cat litter. (That last task was worth me doing everything else in exchange.) There was a new set of keys dangling from the ignition, a different mailbox with *our* names on it and a sweet light shining from a little house in Laurel Canyon…Laurel Canyon the woodsy West Coast alternative to Bleecker Street, home and inspiration to countless legendary musicians of the '60s and '70s, including Carole King, Graham Nash, and Neil Young, author of "Cowgirl in the Sand."

Adam and I were the missing pieces to each others' puzzles, not magnets that repelled. We became true BFFs, staunch supporters of each others' endeavors. We would have our daughter Layla three years later and get married six years after that. Layla would be very excited about the wedding. I would know this because when I went to pick her up from school the day before, the maintenance man congratulated me.

I don't know if the *antidote* theory is true, but it sure *feels* true. Alex broke up with her tormented actor and married a grounded auto technician. We are both in the process of living happily ever after.

Russell found his *antidote* too. He doubled down on what he always wanted and found somebody who *could* give him 100%. He married her and moved into the beautiful house directly next door to the beautiful house *we* lived in. I'm not kidding. They have three children. I talk to Russell twice a year—on his birthday and on mine. He still makes me laugh.

P.S. Adam's Dad, Al Gorgoni, has had a diverse and noteworthy career in the music business. He was a session guitarist on countless No.1 records in the '60s and '70s. He wrote, "I Can't Let Go" for Linda Ronstadt and played on "The Sounds of Silence." And also? He came up with that legendary guitar motif on "Brown Eyed Girl." You know the one. He was paid $60 for that session. Never got any songwriting credit.

A Visit from Jim

WHEN ADAM AND I were first dating, he was getting busy composing soundtracks, but he had a pretty good three-minute songwriting instinct as well. So once in a while (before he discovered how bossy I could be), we would collaborate. That is, when we were on the same coast. I was still living in N.Y. and he was living in L.A. Fortunately, "bicoastability" was feasible in our line of work.

On one of my visits west we asked our fun-loving friend and L.A. songwriting staple, Phil Roy, to join us for a *SongSex ménage à trois*. We knew we'd have a good time and maybe we'd even get around to writing a song.

Phil showed up all burly and cheerful with his plastic green-yellow-red-blue Fisher-Price tape-recorder, a tiny microphone attached to it by a rubber coil. The juxtaposition of him with this child's toy was amusing, but when we got to working it was a good thing he brought it along because his asymmetric, unrepeatable, staccato verses came out in one fell swoop—we wouldn't have remembered a thing had it not been documented. Beautiful mistakes happen all the time and disappear into thin air never to be heard from again. It doesn't matter how low tech your gadget is, as long as it works.[1]

---

[1] Voice Memos on mobile devices have made it a no-brainer to save bits and pieces of ideas. You can name them, edit them, sync them, and share them. Still, sometimes it was less complicated to just press "record" on a child's toy.

I had become obsessed with the first two chord changes in the hook of Don Henley's "Heart of the Matter" (a simple I chord to a ii minor 11th). So why not try them out on the song we were writing? It's all trial and error anyway. You don't know for sure how anything will sound, until you release it from your curiosity and bring it forth into the ether. You have to start somewhere.

After those first two changes, Adam took over. (I never hesitate to have someone else play if they play better, or differently. It keeps me from defaulting to the same familiar patterns.) The three of us bounced lines and melodies around until the song was finished. Much fun was had in the process. A song *always* turns out better when you're having a good time writing it.

The following week we recorded a demo. Phil asked if he could bring his friend Jim to the session. Jim was all bummed out because he had just broken up with his girlfriend. He and Phil were going out afterwards, so it would be convenient for them to be together. Adam lived in a modest ground floor apartment in the flats of West Hollywood. The dining room *was* his studio. There was a futon in an adjacent living room where Jim could hang, but no wall separating the space. So, naturally, our concern…

What if Jim was chatty and distracting? What if he was a pain in the ass?

What the hell. We said, "Okay."

When they showed up, we handed Jim a beer, a landline and pointed the way to the restroom in case he needed to use it. He promised to stay on the futon and be quiet.

We had hired seasoned pro, Lisa Frazier, who came over and belted out a lead. No Auto-Tune required. That meant she really had to sing. Then it was time for some background vocals and Phil said,

"Jim's a pretty good singer. Why doesn't he sing some 'BV's' with us?"

Seriously? Are you trying to cheer him up? He doesn't look all that depressed.

We gave Jim a pair of headphones, but his singing was a little off and we sent him back to the futon. He had this curious goofy smile on his face, like it was no big deal. At least we hadn't hurt his feelings. At the end of the session, Phil and Jim went on their merry way.

The next morning while Adam was still asleep, I walked around the corner and brought back some bagels and a newspaper. As I spread the entertainment section on the living room floor to check out what movies were playing that night, a very familiar face caught my eye. In living color (no pun intended)…it was the guy we told to shut up and stay on the futon. *Ace Ventura: Pet Detective* was opening *that* weekend.

"Umm, Adam…Wake up."

It occurred to us that Phil had, in fact, mentioned his friend Jim had a gig on some TV show. But this was L.A., *everyone* had a gig on some TV show. Looking back, Phil must have thought, "*Wow, Adam and Shelly are cool…not fawning all over Jim like everyone does. Treating him like a normal guy. Come to think of it, treating him a little like shit.*"

That said, in a matter of a week or two, Jim wouldn't be able to go anywhere without being followed or photographed. So it might have been nice for him to go some place where nobody knew his name, or face, or goofy smile.

Adam on the futon to which Jim was banished. I would have taken a photo with Jim on it, but we didn't know it was Jim. Note the mic in the dining room in the foreground. The song we wrote that day, "Even if It Breaks My Heart," was recorded by Cliff Richard.

The Opportunists

PHIL (ROY) ALWAYS seemed to be living somewhere unconventional…in a castle in Beachwood Canyon in Hollywood, in an art gallery at Bergamot Station in Santa Monica. At this particular point in time, he was living on a friend's houseboat in Marina del Rey. Adam and I were invited over on a sunny Saturday afternoon. Jim was there, as well as a handful of Phil's eclectic comrades. Needless to say, Jim's career had taken off since we last saw him. He was preparing for a new movie called *Dumb and Dumber* (the original) and he was sporting that ridiculous *Dumb and Dumber* haircut.

The gathering got going. Wine was served. A joint was passed, and then Phil took out his guitar. It didn't take long before something started "happening." This wasn't the usual one-on-one collaboration or even the occasional three-way. This was an orgy. Everyone was sitting in a circle throwing out contributions—very chaotic and spontaneous. For some reason, every line was awesome. It wasn't the plan to write a song that day, but sometimes they just materialize.

This one was a rather ambitious endeavor…the concept being: *we all want to be rock stars but not everyone can handle the fame.* We called it "Overdose and Die." It's not funny, I *know.* But at the time we all thought it was. Because you know what happens when you're stoned…everything seems like it's so much *more* than whatever it is. If it's blue, it's bluer. If you're hungry, you're starving. If it has *some* humor, it's *hilarious.* And if you're writing a song, it's brilliant, and maybe it *was* a little brilliant (or prophetic at least) because we used Michael Jackson and Kurt Cobain as examples of celebrities that were destroyed by fame. And sadly, this was long before they were.

Driving home later that night, Adam and I saw the possibilities. We had just written a *brilliant* song with the hottest new star in Hollywood. Being the celebrity that he was, certainly he'd be in a position to use the piece in one of his films. With a *big fat* synchronization (usage) fee attached. I closed my eyes and saw us on the red carpet at an *Ace Ventura* sequel. I envisioned our names next to Jim's as the music credits rolled. What we *needed* was a demo so he'd have something to share with a director. And, we needed to record one fast while the song was still fresh in our minds.

So we made a plan. We'd get up bright and early and start working on it. I'd call Phil and ask him to ask Jim to come sing it…in the same apartment where he had been banished to the futon. But the Universe must have been paying us back for being such shameful opportunists, because in the morning we couldn't remember how the song went. What were the words? Did anyone write them down? Where was the green-yellow-red-blue Fisher Price tape recorder when we needed it and why wasn't it there yesterday?

Adam and I called Phil in a panic. He faxed over his handwritten notes, which were illegible except for a few lines here and there. We squinted and held them up to the light. What does that say? Why couldn't Phil have better penmanship? When we finally put enough of the pieces together, and were honest with ourselves, we realized the blue was just, well, blue. Beige even. The hilarity? Not so funny. The potential? Gone. The song was simply unexceptional in every way.

C'est la vie. I make no excuses. A serial songwriter *must* always look for opportunities to try to make things happen, because sometimes we *can*. If we can't, well, we'd better have fun trying. Because very often, all we get is the fantasy.

P.S. Layla, my child, if you're reading this, yes it's true, I smoked pot on occasion. But my prefrontal cortex was more developed than yours is now. And? I was lucky. I could stop. Some people can't. And you might be one of them. So don't do drugs.

And while we're on the subject, full disclosure…I also smoked my share of cigarettes. When I was stressed out or when someone broke up with me. If I was desperate, I might have retrieved a soggy butt from the bottom of the trash. I was young and gross. I did things I implore you not to do. Nobody is worth it.

On the boat: Nicholas Klein, Me, Adam, Deirdre O'Hara (Phil's publisher at the time), Phil, Jim Carrey.

Wilson (No) Phillips

I CUT MY finger on a kitchen knife slicing watermelon. I was a little nervous. I am always a little nervous before a writing session. No matter what. No matter who. Will they like me? Will I live up to their expectations? Will I be on my game? I wrapped my stinging thumb in a paper towel and secured it with a rubber band. The doorbell rang. There was Carnie Wilson, an armful of journals, ponytail bobbing atop her head, flustered, as if she wanted to tell me something immediately. She didn't even know me. She hadn't even walked through the door.

Hit & Run had arranged this collaboration. They were coming through with their promise of getting me in the room with recording artists. Of course I knew of Carnie from the vocal trio, Wilson Phillips, which consisted of Carnie, her sister Wendy, (daughters of legendary Beach Boy, Brian Wilson) and Chynna Phillips (daughter of John and Michelle Phillips of The Mamas & the Papas). When they came onto the scene back in 1990, rumor had it Wilson Phillips was going to sell 10 million records. Record labels often say things like that when they want to create a buzz. Valerie Block and I had written a song called "Live with Pride" and SBK, their record label, loved it and had the girls record it with renowned producer, Glen Ballard. We were beside ourselves.

There was a caveat: whether or not it would make the final cut was contingent upon us handing over 50% of the ownership of the song (half the royalties) to SBK's sister publishing company. Val was okay with it. I, on the other hand, saw it as extortion. I called their bluff. It wasn't a bluff. They did not include it on the album, which went on to sell over 10 million copies worldwide. That would have earned Val and me almost half a million dollars in album sales alone even *after* "extortion." That was a lot of money, especially in 1990. Being on that album would have catapulted us into the major leagues. "Live with Pride" never made a cent. (I'm so sorry, Val, though you look very happy on Facebook.)

Six years later, Carnie walked into my home and got right down to the business of what was on her mind. Let's just say there was drama. I loved how Carnie's heart was on her sleeve from the ring of the bell. Emotions melting off the surface, looking for someone to receive them…a sure sign there would be plenty of "Song Fodder." And it wasn't all about her. She was interested in me, my life. Why the paper towel and the rubber band?

Sister, Wendy, followed shortly. Sweet, warm, not as dramatic. That was probably a good thing. Two Carnies might have been too much. There would be no Chynna as it was Carnie and Wendy's record for which we were writing, but it *was* going to be a foursome as Glen Burtnik, a super talented, upbeat, songwriter extraordinaire would be joining us.

I don't think we actually got down to writing on day one. I have a photo of us in my living room, kicking back and laughing about something Glen said. That's how it was back then. You got to know with whom you were working. You kissed before you fucked. It's called "foreplay." We weren't in a rush. Artists collaborated with a handful of writers for an upcoming album, not dozens. Thoughts were intimate. Time spent was quality. Watermelon was served.

While we yapped and kvetched and vented and shared, I, the clandestine secretary, took note of our confessions, affirmations, and promises to ourselves, so that when we were ready to get down to business, we'd have an arsenal of concepts from which to draw. It's not like I was being sneaky. On the contrary—the most authentic material comes from these personal exchanges and I knew that. So did they. Sometimes the process of writing a song starts before you are actually doing it.

As the most agile musician, Glen was our captain. He was tireless and never lost his sense of humor, even with three spirited women squawking in his ear. Over the course of that week (yes a whole week), we wrote five songs. One of my favorites was "Open Door," which might have been a metaphor for Carnie's hope that someone would walk through hers...or maybe for how she and Wendy walked through *mine*. In any event, somebody somewhere was being welcomed (I like to think that life seeps into art). The other was "One Bright Day," a song about life being short and walls being built and maybe one (bright) day "we'll climb over." Glen sang the lead on the demo in his best Brian Wilson and the girls sang Beach Boys-esque harmonies. Carnie's wish was for her Dad to hear it and be so moved that he'd record it himself. (Needless to say, Glen and I had no objection to that.) I remember her calling her Dad and telling him how excited she was about the song. She gave him the demo, but I don't know what he said or if he ever heard it.

I loved everything about Carnie...her excitability, her no bullshit, her haunting and honest singing voice. There are no plug-ins for that.

Here are other things I remember from that week:

- Carnie and Wendy co-wrote a lot of the songs on that first Wilson Phillips record (the one that sold 10 million), but told me they blew their small fortune on aromatherapy and scented candles. I'm not sure if they were kidding. I thought of all the candles I could have bought with the royalties I never made from "Live with Pride."

- Carnie confessed she had been through some hurtful times. She was a beautiful young woman—eyes alive and sparkling. But it was an MTV world where you could no longer tell the difference between a pop star and a supermodel, and Carnie struggled with her weight. In the Wilson Phillips videos, you'd see a full length Wendy and Chynna, but a Carnie from shoulders up. Or Wendy and Chynna in sexy strappy dresses, and Carnie wrapped in a boxy jacket with excess material, or she'd be in the background, or not on camera at all. She showed us one video where her head was simply floating around the screen in a bubble. How demoralizing it must have been.

- We collectively discovered the delight of frozen grapes.

Glen and I never made much money from the work we did with Carnie and Wendy. You'll never hear the songs we wrote, unless you search for them on Japanese imports. Sales were considerably less than 10 million, but that's okay. The week was well spent. I met people I will never forget... people who cared and wanted to be cared about. Life is what happens when you're busy trying to write songs that make money. From every songwriting session that you enter, hopefully you give something away and take something with you when you leave. It's not always a paycheck or a Gold record.

Kissing before SongSex. Carnie, Wendy and Glen.

Daring to Suck

I HAVE A writing session mantra: "Dare to Suck." I honestly can't remember if I made it up or heard it somewhere. I noticed Ke$ha referred to it in an interview. I definitely did *not* get it from Ke$ha, as I'd been using it quite a while before she was doing interviews, perhaps even before she was born. Some say it was I who coined the phrase and it made its way around the block. That's okay with me.

Anyway, "Dare to Suck" is this: Be willing to make a fool of yourself, because if you're only offering up the safe stuff, chances are it will be boring. Think of it this way—when you're writing a song, your unconscious brain is at work. Perhaps something about your clumsy word or thought—the vowel sound, the flavor of the idea, if you will—has logic to it and there is a reason it occurred to you. As embarrassing as it is to say out loud, you must do so, as the energy of your clumsy word or thought may steer your *co-writer* to a more agreeable or interesting word or thought. Like "fruity" to "beauty" for example, or "kumquat" to "love knot."

It goes without saying that you have to feel comfortable enough with the people you work with to "DTS." Hopefully, they won't start tweeting about what a lame writer you are while you're sitting right there next to them. And, reciprocally, they have to trust you with *their* clumsy words or thoughts. Hopefully, they will have some.

That Song!

IT WASN'T LONG after making the move to Los Angeles, that I, The Eternal Optimist, almost stopped believing I would ever have a hit song. Contemporaries all around were getting lucky. I had been at it for nearly ten years. My work appeared on dozens of albums worldwide and had been recorded by big-time artists like Celine Dion and Regina Belle. But I had never had a hit...a song that gets released to radio and goes viral—a song that changes your life. A song that negates all the past rejection and instantly upgrades your status from good to great. A song you can finally refer to when you're at that party and get asked that dreaded question..."*Have you written anything I'd know?*" Seriously, I was considering going back to waitressing, because when you're standing at that table at least you're in control. The diners are at your mercy, even though they may be millionaires, and all you have is a checking account. Waitressing was empowering and I needed some power because I was feeling pretty dejected.

There was something else on my mind as well. Now that I had found someone I wanted to spend my life with, the idea of having a baby was becoming more agreeable. Exciting even. And, let's be frank...in my late thirties, how many more times could I smack that snooze button? If I kept waiting for "That Song," I could be waiting a long time. Then maybe it would be too late.

On the other hand, without *that song* (or "*that film*"), I wondered if Adam and I would be able to maintain our modest but comfortable lifestyle. After all the baby paraphernalia, the college fund and the nanny, would we still be able to afford to take a vacation now and then? Go out for sushi on Friday nights? Buy health insurance? More frightening than the financial concern was the idea that creativity would have a different place in my life with a baby on board. Impulses I was always able to address as soon as I had them would have to wait.

We ended up doing what most couples do when they're scared shitless—go for it anyway. After all, our lives were about more than the trajectory of our careers. We were in love. We *wanted* a child. We would make it work. Of course we would—*that song* or not.

Just as we came to that realization, and as I was about to head over to the Cheesecake Factory to fill out an application, artist manager Lori Leve introduced me to Meredith Brooks. Meredith had been trying to get a record deal and had been having *SongSex* with a number of writers hoping they could help her find *her* magic. Why hadn't it happened yet?

With measured expectations I went to see Meredith's showcase at The Mint, only to find…this chick could rock! And pipes? She had those too. I could tell she was *not* going to take no for an answer. Some people might call that obnoxious. I call it a necessary ingredient for getting what one wants. My kind of girl. In my mind, she just needed…*that song*.

A week or so later I was driving home from a writing session with a severe case of PMS, smoking what was perhaps my last "occasional" cigarette of all time, as I was, in fact, soon to be pregnant. I stopped at a red light on the corner of Magnolia and Lankershim in North Hollywood, took another drag and had what turned out to be a life-changing thought:

I hate the world today…Adam is going to have to deal with my dark side when I get home. Poor guy, I can be such a bitch.

Then it hit me, and the light turned green.

Now I could so easily have stepped on the gas and advanced to the next red light. I could have had that thought and gone on to another without ever skipping a beat. But I'm a songwriter. So I didn't. I caught it. Songwriters have to be able to recognize golden nuggets—when something they hear or say to themselves is song-worthy. Material is all around us—inside and out, like low-hanging fruit on tree branches. We have to be ready to pluck those ripe juicy apples.

I called Meredith in the morning and shared the idea with her. I had a hunch she knew what it was like to be that bitch. There's an added benefit to writing with someone who shares your point of view: you don't have to put words in her (or his) mouth. She said she'd be right over.

We wrote a song (minus the very last line of the hook) in about an hour on Meredith's acoustic guitar in the tiny bedroom-slash-office of my Laurel Canyon home. No amplifiers or keyboards. My line, her line—two girls in a bubble without a beat, batting it back and forth. It was *outstanding SongSex.* The best I ever had with a woman. Maybe the best I've ever had period. We had a feeling something went right that day. She more than I, but I was used to being wrong.

That afternoon Meredith phoned in the last line:

You know you wouldn't want it any other way.

Later she would tell me it occurred to her as she drove away from my house. (The best lines *often* reveal themselves when you're driving away. It has something to do with the letting go, the letting be, the not forcing. A last line—the summing up—is more likely to surrender itself when it's not being sought after with fierce determination. This isn't a matter of will. It is spiritual.)

Her line was perfect. At the time, however, I thought it was just okay. To me it sounded like we couldn't think of anything better. As I said, I was used to being wrong.

Before I could blink, Meredith vanished into the recesses of an adjacent canyon and reappeared the very next day with a blazing demo she recorded with her producer friend Geza-X. The rest happened in a flash. She played it for Lori, who played it on a car stereo for Perry Watts Russell, A&R (artist & repertoire) at Capitol Records. Perry signed Meredith to a record deal the following day with "Bitch" as *that song,* to be released as soon as they could get all the ducks in order. I braced for disappointment.

They say babies bring bread. I couldn't agree more, because about six months later, I was driving down the hill in my little Miata, pregnant belly up against the steering wheel, when I heard a familiar drum loop on KROQ radio. I couldn't quite place it. Then I heard, "I hate the world today," and there it was. Surreal.

I should have pulled over and enjoyed the moment. Hugged myself. But I wasn't thinking clearly. I felt like I had to tell someone. I had to tell *everyone*. It was 1997, the year of that Motorola cell phone that was the size of a shoe. There were more charges for dropped calls than for connections, especially in the canyon. I tried my Mom; it went to her answering machine. I called Joey at Hit & Run, who had been picking up my option for years. He deserved to know. As I panted my announcement, the reception fizzled in and out. He knew I was excited about something, he just couldn't figure out what. I called my sister, my best friend, and my baby-daddy. I could not connect. I gave up, and just as I did, *that song* was fading out and the next one was fading in. So replaceable—interchangeable—fleeting. The moment was gone.

There will always be writers with another *that song* on the radio every week. For me, it's a precious three minutes, and from that day on, any time a song of mine is played anywhere, I give it my undivided attention. I savor it like there may never be another.

Corner of La Brea and Beverly. (Look at the price of gasoline!)

"Bitch" video shoot. I was 5 months pregnant. Clockwise: Janet Gunn, Beth ?, Me, Meredith Brooks, Victoria Levy, Joan Schneibel, Pamela Hodes, Diana Nall Browne, Lori Leve.

A Perfect Storm

THERE ARE PIECES of me in every song I've ever written, but "Bitch" was like looking in a mirror. Meredith might have brought it to life, but it was just as much *my song* as it was hers.

There wasn't a line that didn't describe who *I* was, or who I would be shortly. Certainly I *could* be a bitch; even my father knew it. I was definitely a "lover" and soon to be "a mother." As for a "child," there's part of every songwriter that resides in a state of arrested development. That's one of the reasons why we're songwriters. As for a sinner and a saint? I was a Gemini, full of *yin* and *yang*. Lastly, Adam will attest I was his hell *and* his dream. Luckily he really *wouldn't* have wanted it any other way—I don't think.

And how nice, for a change, to invite somebody else into *my* idea, as opposed to being willing (as I had been so many times before and would happily be again) to help *them* with theirs. Still, the song came from the core of Meredith (a fellow Gemini) as well. She meant every word we wrote. It was a 50/50 mix of our DNA—a *SongSex* love child.

There are other songs I've written of which I'm proud and love as much for different reasons. But to have been so true to myself *and* have had commercial success at the same time was a cosmic collaborative collision of art and commerce. Often I have one or the other, but rarely both. For me, I don't know if there will ever be another storm as perfect.

Bitches & Babies

AS "BITCH" WAS rising on the charts and my belly was rising on me, I wrote a short essay called "Bitches and Babies." In the piece, I contemplated how I would feel after becoming a mother. Would I be as obsessed with my career? I hoped not. Would I feel less desperate for validation? I hoped so.

I had remained close with Jesse, the friend I had made at that songwriting workshop in the back room of Uncle Lulu's. We had shared many coming-of-age years together in New York. He was there helping me sweep up the dead roaches after fumigating my 85th Street apartment. He was there hovering over me when I fainted at a Papaya King from a combination of the summer heat and one too many hits of a joint. And, he was there after I had a disastrous rendezvous with an ex-short-term boyfriend who wanted to get back together.

"Ex" had a cocaine habit—the reason for our split. From across a table at the uptown Café Luxembourg, Ex swore he was through with it. But he was fidgety and hyper and he kept excusing himself to go the men's room. More of the same.

I called him out. He hung his head like a naughty little boy that had just gotten caught telling a lie and agreed to surrender the packet of white powder to me under the table. Then he became hostile because he was coming down. So I left the restaurant, and because I knew if I went home, Ex would follow, I cabbed across town to Jesse's. Shaken, I told him what had happened. How pathetic Ex was. I told him about the under-the-table exchange. Jesse's eyes widened, his voice lowered:

"You *have* the coke?" But I digress.

Over the years since we met, Jesse had gone from being an aspiring songwriter himself to a successful journalist. So, when he read "Bitches and Babies," he circulated it on my behalf and, lo and behold, it was published in *She*, a New Zealand women's magazine.

He encouraged me to continue writing. Really? I loved writing. Writing whatever—stories, songs. I got busy as my belly swelled. What could I say about impending motherhood that had never been said? Jesse suggested that continuing to incorporate well-known, self-penned songs and the artists who recorded them into my stories would be the key to getting more of them published. Trouble was, at that point, "Bitch" was my only hit. I *had* no well-known body of work. (And just because you had a hit, doesn't mean rejection stops. It takes a while to accumulate a well-known body of work.)

Not that it would have made a difference. Because when Layla came onto the scene, I fell into a rabbit hole. There was hardly time to floss my teeth much less contribute to another magazine. My stories became a list of ".docs" in a folder buried in the recesses of my computer hard drive. Maybe someday, I would dig them up.

Snapshot: Sara Smile

I'm with Jake swaying back and forth in the dark
to "Sara Smile." Maybe he feels the same way
about me as Daryl (Hall) feels for Sara. Please
God! I've fallen and I can't get up. Every time
the song is over, Jake picks up the needle and
starts it again. I have no idea that for the rest
of my life whenever I hear that iconic motif at
the top of the song, it will be like a little stab in
my heart. He didn't feel the same way at all.

Her Name Was Christina

HOLLYWOOD IS FILLED with thousands of WannaBes. Good singers who will never be great. Great singers who will never be stars. As a songwriter, it helps to be able to tell the difference.

Remarkable things can happen on ordinary days. On one of those ordinary days, Todd Chapman, a fellow songwriter, called to say he was working with an amazing singer. Her name was Christina—Christina Agyasomething. He wanted me to come over and check her out. *That's* what was ordinary. I got that call a lot, like once a week. "This girl can *really* sing." Yeah Yeah Yeah. Blah Blah Blah.

Layla was a few months old at the time. My nipples were sore. My sleep was deprived. Our nanny, Reina, was part time. Needless to say I didn't have the energy or the freedom to drop everything and go everywhere. But *if* I had a hankering to spend time with a particular writing partner, or let's face it, if I had heard a buzz on an amazing singer from other songwriters, I would find a way. I wasn't quitting. I was simply adjusting my gears. Thankfully, I went to Todd's that day.

Todd lived in a nondescript two-story apartment complex in North Hollywood. The block was lined with them. A vacancy sign out front...a wrought iron entrance gate with a lock that wasn't locked...a swimming pool in a concrete courtyard surrounded by plastic chairs and inexpensive potted plants. Poorly lit hallways led to countless doors of studio and one-bedroom units.

I rang a bell and when one of those doors opened, I saw her standing at a mic…waif-like and small chested—her hair un-styled…a Big Mac, fries and a Diet Coke on a table a few feet away. There was nothing particularly striking or glamorous about her. We said, "Hi I'm Shelly/Hi I'm Christina, nice to meet you," and then I plopped myself on the sofa and observed while she and Todd finished recording the song they had been working on. She was soft spoken and didn't express much of an opinion; she sang when Todd asked her to. However, when she opened her mouth? This girl could *really* sing. On a scale of 1 to 10—*this* girl was a 20!

Todd had a relationship with A&R exec Ron Fair who intended to make an album with Christina, an ex-Mouseketeer. (The recording industry was having considerable luck with them.) It wasn't uncommon for label execs to ask aspiring producers to work with prospective artists to get an idea of how compatible they'd be and to make sure the artist had studio chops. Potentially, a couple of those original songs could wind up on the forthcoming album, if and when it got made. As it turned out, *this* ex-Mouseketeer was was extremely composed and had studio chops on steroids.

Over the next month or so, Christina graced a few songs that Todd and I wrote with her amazing voice. We kept the McDonalds coming.

Meanwhile, on another very ordinary day, I pumped some breast milk, waited for Reina, and then went over to The Banana Boat Recording Studio, about a mile away from Todd's place, to work with Guy Roche, another up and coming producer and go-to collaborator. There was no artist in particular for whom we were writing. We were doing it simply for the joy of *SongSex* and we'd deal with the casting later. In 1998, if you came up with a quality song, chances were it would find a home. I pressed record on my handheld cassette player and Guy started free styling on a keyboard, which prompted me to excavate for a receipt from my wallet, because I remembered scribbling some words on it the day before. They were about Adam giving me space when I wasn't sure about moving to L.A. Like a rock, Adam waited patiently while I got it together and figured it out. Sound familiar? I wish I were the kind of writer who could make stuff up day after day and turn it into hits. For me, the best material has always been inspired by real life.

As we were working on the hook-in-progress, I got disoriented and sang it in a slightly different pocket the second time through: on the downbeat instead of as a pickup. When we listened back to our work tape, we agreed that we liked that mistake. Some happy accidents are keepers!

That's kinda hooky, I suspected. *Let's see if it still feels hooky in the morning.* That's always a good test. Is it the first thing you think about—before coffee or a kiss?

I went home, paid Reina, gave Layla a bath, blew raspberries on her belly, her tush, her feet, delighted in her giggle, pumped some more milk and handed her over to Adam who gave her a bottle, read her *Goodnight Moon,* rocked her until her eyes closed, and then, very carefully so as not to wake her up, lowered our sleeping baby into her crib. I made us some dinner, watched "Sex in the City" and then, like an eager puppy, jumped onto the bed where Adam was reading. I tossed him a pair of headphones and asked him to have a listen. He was not a pushover, and he wasn't that into Top 40. *That's* why it mattered. He agreed with the one word. *Hooky.* That was enough for me. He went back to his book. I was thrilled.

The next week, Guy and I recorded a demo of our song, "What a Girl Needs." In retrospect, it was rather lethargic. We must have pitched it to at least twenty-five artists and A&R departments. They all passed. But when Guy's manager played that demo for Ron Fair, *he* heard the potential and thought Christina should record it for her debut album. Fantastic!

But Uh-oh…What to tell Todd? He was the one who invited me to the "Christina party." After all the time we spent with her, Ron likes THIS song… one that I didn't write with Todd. But, like I said, you can't control this stuff.

My response to Ron? "That's fantastic! When will she cut it?" First things first. Ron wanted us to make a change. The hook began, "What a girl needs, what a girl wants." He was adamant we switch the order of the "needs" and the "wants." His feeling was that the "wants" wasn't so *needy,* and therefore better front and center, and the alliteration of the "whats" and the "wants" was ear candy.

He has a point. But if I make that swap, I'll have to change the whole rhyme scheme in the hook. On the upside, I might get my song on the album.

I made the swap.

I'm not sure eighteen-year-old Christina realized what was ahead of her at the time, but she didn't seem fazed about stepping into the spotlight… going from mouse ears to bustiers. She came out of the bottle, I mean the gate, with her first single, "Genie in a Bottle," which went straight to No. 1. I was so envious of my friend, Pam Sheyne, one of the writers of "Genie," I could have died. But I'm glad I didn't because the momentum of "Genie" propelled the second single, "What a Girl Wants" (not needs) onto the Hot 100 where it spent 24 weeks.

I remember Christina being obsessed with Mariah Carey. Not surprisingly, between her pipes and her moxie she would reach heights equal to the superstar. I can only imagine what a rollercoaster ride it's been for her. The 0 to 60 superstardom. The many hits versus the few flops, the marriage, the divorce, going from being a baby herself to having some of her own, the weight fluctuations, the tan, the breasts, the hair extensions. I watched a polished and articulate Christina radiate as a judge on "The Voice" and couldn't believe she was the same shy little girl in Todd's apartment. The one with the thin blonde hair. The one with no opinion. The one I never could have imagined, when I opened the door on that very ordinary day, would be the driver who would escort my little ditty to the top of the charts.

P.S. Christina must have realized how lucky she was to have a committed advocate in Ron Fair, because if you crank up the fade at the end of the song you can hear her ad-libbing: "I turn to Ron Fair whenever you're not there." I don't know who it was that wasn't there, but apparently Ron would be a fine stand-in if they didn't show.

Ron Fair, Christina, me.

Miss America

IF YOU GOOGLE me, something might come up that I haven't mentioned. I was in the Miss America Pageant in 1979. That's right. A girl from Long Island was able to represent the state of Maryland, if she went to school there, and I did. You may wonder what relevance this has to my career in the music business. It doesn't, but the experience taught me that some of life's more puzzling detours are just as instrumental in helping us find out who we are as some of the more obvious roads.

Full disclosure: when I was little, I watched "Miss America," and "Miss USA," and "Miss Universe"—Miss Anything. Cozied up in my parents' bed, foil on the tips of the TV antenna, bag of Fritos by my side, I rated the contestants with a pencil and clipboard in hand. Very official.

In high school, I happily participated in some local pageants. It was part of our culture to celebrate women for their appearance. It wasn't until I took a couple of women's studies classes in college that I started realizing how objectifying this was. But it would take more than a couple of classes to undo what was ingrained in me as a child.

It certainly wasn't my goal to be in the Miss America Pageant, but when I was in a Greek life production of *The Princess and the Pea*, a few of the local Jaycees (sort of like the grown-up Boy Scouts) were in the audience hoping to recruit a few young women for a preliminary pageant for Miss

Maryland. When the Jaycees approached *me* after the show, I was flattered. I said, "Why not," I'd compete.

Somehow I won that local competition, which then put me in the state competition. Then I won the state competition, and became Miss Maryland. Before I knew it, I was on one big runaway train without any brakes. I began getting migraines. Bad ones. Something didn't feel right. Maybe I didn't really want to *be* Miss America after all.

It was too late. There was no turning back. What a mess I would make if I did. Like a good girl, I spent the summer with my sponsors (Jaycee "Jack" and his wife "Liv") keeping up with current events, rehearsing my talent and practicing squeezing my legs together so that when I stood half naked before the judges in the swimsuit competition there would be contact from the top of my inner thighs to my ankles…no light shining through anywhere. This was a must on the Miss America prototype checklist. In September, I was off to Atlantic City.

In the pre-telecast swimsuit competition, all the leg squeezing paid off and with pads in my bra cups, I excelled. I was one of three swimsuit winners. According to Pageant aficionados and historical statistics, this put me in a very favorable position. One of the three swimsuit winners almost always took the crown.

The local Jaycees and their wives were beside themselves at the thought of my prospects. If I won it would be a first for the little state of Maryland (they had never had a winner), and I felt a huge responsibility to come through for my sponsors. The migraines got worse. How counterintuitive to be in a contest that I didn't want to win. I smeared Vaseline on my teeth and smiled through the panic.

As the pre-televised activities continued, my advantage started to wane. In my interview with the judges, I was asked about my thoughts on the Ayatollah Khomeini, the price of oil, Three Mile Island and yes, world peace. Of course I *was* for world peace, but even with all my studying up I wasn't a rocket scientist, and when it came to the Ayatollah or nuclear reactors, the judges found that out quickly. Next…

In the talent competition, I accompanied myself on the piano (the largest and shiniest I'd ever seen) while I sang a somber, self-penned ballad called "Carry Me Home." I had written it over the summer while contemplating my trepidations about going to Atlantic City. It had a "*what have I gotten myself into*" tone to it that wasn't as subtle as I had hoped. Truth is, I could have sung something a bit more glitzy and optimistic. I could have lost the piano and diva'd my heart out in all the glory chiffon and sequins would allow. But number one, I did not possess the necessary vibrato. And number two, like I said…*I didn't actually want to win.*

On the night the show aired, not only didn't I win, I wasn't even in the top ten. Never have I been so embarrassed and so relieved at the same time. The migraines subsided.

The relief alone made me realize how stressful it is to try to be someone other people want you to be, and how at times we find out who we are by a *very* painful process of elimination. Sometimes, you have to push back, and not go with anybody else's flow. You have to resist the flattery…or just *be* flattered but say "no thank you." This is *your* life.

I spent the remainder of that year proudly representing the state of Maryland by attending grand openings, cutting ribbons, visiting veterans' hospitals, riding in parades and doing that wave (you know the one). I didn't mind. I had my life back. At the end of my reign, I hightailed it to New York City to figure out who *I* really wanted to be.

That wave (I made the dress).

P.S. Once, the Baltimore Sun *came to my apartment to interview me. George, my then boyfriend, had stayed over the night before and we overslept. The doorbell rang before he had a chance to exit and before I had a chance to locate my crown and banner (much less a dress). I did that interview in gym shorts, a T-shirt and a bandana on my head. George spent two hours hiding in the dark, crouched under the hanging clothes in my bedroom closet. The* Baltimore Sun *printed a story about the virtues of being a girl-next-door-pageant-contestant, alongside a staged photo of me washing my living room windows.*

Washing windows. (George was in the closet.)
I can't believe I had to pay the Baltimore Sun *$310 for the rights to use this picture of me!*

P.P.S. On one of my appearances as the reigning Miss Maryland, I threw out the first ball to Doug DeCinces at a Baltimore Orioles game. I was asked if I wanted to sing the pre-game National Anthem as well. Flattered as I was, I demurred. I had learned my lesson; I was not that girl.

One on One

IT WAS THE end of the day and I rocked Layla in the dark, contemplating the fluorescent glow of the stars on the ceiling above us. It occurred to me that I had bought those stars when I was still pregnant and had *just* affixed them *that* morning, a year later.

I'd been in perpetual motion since the day she was born—always in a hurry. Trying to accomplish in three hours what it used to take a leisurely week to do—feeling like I'd been functioning with one hand tied behind my back.

I know what you must be thinking: I only had one child. That's true. I often wondered how my friends with two or three were juggling career and motherhood—respect to the max. Still, even when you have just one, from the moment they emerge, your life does not belong to you alone anymore. Any pre-existing obsession with efficiency and productivity must be modulated.

There was enough light for me to see that Layla was contemplating the fluorescent stars as well. She sucked on her bottle while we listened to Raffi.

I can't believe I'm listening to Raffi.

There I was. Actually enjoying the calm. The immobility. The here and now.

As she started becoming heavy lidded from the elixir of warm milk, I realized I was collecting some thoughts. Which were:

1. *Perhaps having a child is the ultimate distraction from having to face the scary fact that we're going to die some day. If we're that occupied, we just don't think about it as much.*

2. *Looking back on the mistakes I've made in my life (so far), I would choose the same ones all over again, because they led me to* this *chair in* this *room with* this *baby.*

3. *Meredith hit the nail on the head when she came up with that last line: I really wouldn't want it any other way.*

Layla was quite content, even though she knew she would soon be lowered into the solitary confinement she considered her crib to be. But she must have sensed my contentment as well and that I was not in any rush. She fell asleep in my arms without protest. I rocked her for a while longer, even though I was free to go.

Human & the Chrissies

I WAS WITH a friend who occasionally says careless things. On this particular afternoon, he did it again. My feelings were hurt. I took advantage of that. It behooves a songwriter to make the most of hurt feelings, because they can lead to a heartfelt, significant song. I excused myself and scribbled some words on a napkin. What would songwriters do without napkins?

A few weeks later, I had a songwriting blind date with Mark McEntee of the Australian band, Divinyls, another collaboration arranged by Hit & Run. I loved their song, "I Touch Myself" and spent many an evening dancing to it in my underwear—Tom Cruise *Risky Business*-style. The thought of working with someone I was already a fan of was especially thrilling.

When Mark arrived he was spaced out and undisciplined, but an extremely tasty guitar player...a delicious partner with whom to merge. He wasn't the type of musician who sat in a room every day trying to conjure something commercial (like me). This was a chance to step out of my box and into his careless world. Mark came right at me with a major 7th chord—a songwriting aphrodisiac if I ever heard one. I am infatuated with major 7ths. Never heard one I didn't like. There's a romantic whimsy to them. They create a longing for resolution. Now I was, dare I say it, seduced. Like lovemaking, you move with your partner. You may not be good in bed with everyone, but when you *are* with someone you're good with, you groove together, lock into each other's rhythm, you take their cues and they yours. You might hold a thought back until you feel them shift, but *when* they shift you just know what to say. Not to worry—his or her adept sensibilities will accommodate yours, because you are lovers, at least for that day, for that song. Needless to say, it was a delectable blind date. The words I had written on that napkin weeks earlier found a home in Mark's major 7th heaven.

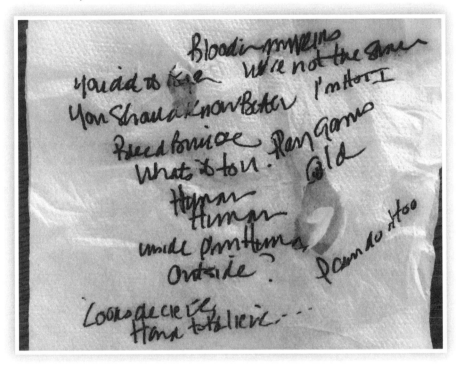

I bleed and I bruise,
But what's it to you…
I'm only human on the inside.

Thank you, hurt feelings.

After spending two days in the studio finding the best tempo, the right drum feel, laying down guitars, recording vocals (no hired guns this time— it was me on the mic and Mark doing background vocals) and then finally mixing our demo, the two of us headed east on Santa Monica Boulevard in that little white convertible. We loaded the CD into the dash and played our song over and over as if to make sure it was as magical as we thought it was. We were an odd couple—the cheerleader and the lost boy—the wind making a mess of our hair…me singing at the top of my lungs and Mark nodding and smiling with subdued satisfaction. He was very pleased with himself.

I THOUGHT FOR sure, BMG, Divinyl's record label, would hear "Human on the Inside," adore it, and include it on their forthcoming album, and that the sheer power of the song would find its way without me having to lift a finger. But Mark returned to Australia and I didn't hear a peep. Eventually, I got news that the album was finished. Panicked, I called Grant Thomas, Mark's manager, who said he had never even heard it. Perhaps Mark went back Down Under and re-entered the same spaced-out cloud he was in before he left. What was I thinking?

I immediately FedExed Grant a copy on a DAT (digital audio tape, circa the 1990s.) Everyone loved it. They held up the release in order to add "Human on the Inside" to the album. I was the poster child for *The Alchemist*—when you believe in something so strongly, the Universe conspires with you to make it happen. Alas, despite all this believing and alchemy (*and* Chrissy Amphlett's[1] seductive vocals), the finished production semi-charted in Australia and quickly faded away.

After this kind of unfortunate reception, a song usually becomes obsolete. It can be tricky to interest another artist in it down the line, unless that artist is very secure and feels like he or she can make it his or her own.

Never say never. Why? Because, not too long after the end of its first life, BMI's Linda Livingston played "Human on the Inside" for rock goddess Chrissie Hynde's agent, Barbara Skydel.[2] Simultaneously, Jon Crawley (Hit & Run, London), who happened to have gone to nursery school with Chrissie's manager, Gail Colson, played it for *her*, while, unbeknownst to anyone, a U.K. songwriter pal, who happened to be friendly with Chrissie's interior decorator, supposedly put a copy in *his* hands (talk about alchemy). I pictured him slipping the cassette into a boom box while measuring for

---

[1] Rest peacefully, Chrissie Amphlett.

[2] And Barbara Skydel.

curtains, and Chrissie poking her head out of the kitchen saying, "What's *that?*"

I will never know for sure which scenario made it come to fruition. Everyone believed it was his or her effort that sealed the deal. Perhaps it was cumulative. Maybe after Chrissie heard it enough she said, "All right, already! I'll record the damn song." (If I ever have a sit down with her, I'm sure she'd have a much less elaborate rendition of how it all came to pass— that the various scenarios, especially the one about the decorator, got misreported and further distorted in a massive game of "telephone." Whatever the case I like to think it was fate.)

In "Hyndesight," I am honored that so many people actively tried to make that record happen. I hadn't asked them all to get involved. In some cases, it wasn't part of their job description to pitch my songs, and, they weren't going to profit personally. They simply *loved* this song, and that was enough.

A few months later I received a copy of Chrissie Hynde—legend, writer of her own colossal hits—singing my words…"*I bleed and I bruise, but what's it to you…I'm only human on the inside.*" I had had many songs recorded before by very notable artists, but this one took the cake. And again, I went driving, by myself this time, playing it over and over, hoping that this was for real…praying I wouldn't wake up and realize it was all a dream.

THE PRETENDERS WERE performing at Lillith Fair that year. Linda Livingston and Barbara Skydel picked me up in a limo and we headed to the concert where they were to play my song in front of tens of thousands of people. Not only did they perform it, Chrissie announced my name to the massive crowd. Imagine…a rock star of her stature taking the time to give someone *else* writing cred during a huge spectacle like that. The performance went by too fast, as it always does. I could barely make out the words in the echo of that huge arena, but it didn't matter.

I took a lot of pictures. From my vantage point, Chrissie was a speck on the stage, barely recognizable. But *I* would know who she was. Linda warned me to save some film for later or I wouldn't have any left for my photo-op with Chrissie. I assured her I had plenty of film. But, after the concert, in Chrissie's trailer, as Linda said, "Say cheese," there was a devastating camera malfunction, for although I had *five* extra rolls of film, I only had *one* battery, and it died. So today, on a shelf in my office, behind my desk, is a framed picture of Chrissie Hynde sitting next to what appears to be me…but actually it's my head cut and pasted atop someone else's torso. Miraculously, my dark hair blends into the dark background and from a distance you'd never know it was rigged. We look very happy together.

Chrissie and me…cut and pasted.

Friends of mine have offered to Photoshop the image so that my head and torso are seamlessly fused, but I prefer my scrappy version as a reminder that for me, a song and its journey have a mind of their own. Though most of those journeys do not turn out as I might have imagined, once in a while, they turn out pretty damn great.

Christina—The Sequel

AS MUCH AS remarkable things can happen on ordinary days, it's equally true that absolutely nothing may happen on days when extraordinary is crucial.

After the success of Christina Aguilera's debut album, Guy Roche and I had the opportunity to write *with* her for her second album. This was *not* an ordinary day. Christina was now a superstar and a lot would ride on the session if we came up with something remarkable. The pressure was on, so I might have been over-thinking, or under-thinking, because my radar went askew.

Christina brought forth a lyric from her journal. It started: "Miss Independence this…Miss Independence that." I dismissed it, as I thought it was amateurish and we wrote a very unremarkable ballad, courtesy of *my* journal, which never saw the light of day.

Christina went on to write that Miss Independence idea with someone else and "Miss Indepen*dent*" became a *big fat hit* for Kelly Clarkson. I told myself that if *we* had written it, we'd have made different choices—written a different song. Perhaps *not* that *big fat hit*, but it didn't make me feel better about my misplaced radar. Curiously, Christina didn't record that "independence song" either, so maybe I wasn't the only one who underestimated it. How it got to Kelly, I'm not sure. There are various accounts of the story, but *some*body saw the potential and sent it. I hope they got a promotion.

Cars & Cats

ON THE DAY the new owners came to pick up my Miata, or 3-JIMMY-340, as she had affectionately become known (her license plate read 3JMY340), I was beside myself. I couldn't bear to go to the door to meet them and hand over the title. Adam did it for me. Bless him. I was in another room cowering in denial.

As much as I lobbied for keeping 3-JIMMY-340, I knew it wasn't practical. It wouldn't be safe for me to be shifting a stick while handing sippy cups and mini boxes of raisins to a toddler. Besides, the Miata was a two-seater, and I had a baby! I was going to need a back seat.

I had test driven a number of "mom" cars and finally chose a blue Jeep Cherokee. Nothing could ever take the place of 3-JIMMY, so I opted for the opposite—something basic and humble. I suppose the *antidote* theory applies to cars as well as lovers.

Things were changing. At social gatherings, Adam and I used to talk about our cats, Sushi and James, when other couples went on about their kids. In our minds, our cats *were* our kids. It wasn't until we had a baby of our own and listened to childless couples go on about Fido (when we spoke of Layla) that we realized what we must have sounded like way back when.

After Layla was born, there were days I'd forget to feed my cherished Sushi, or at least in a timely fashion. When my furry friend became diabetic, Adam had to remind me to give her her daily shot. Once or twice she went into insulin shock and I rushed her to the vet—stiff cat in one arm, sleepy baby in the other. I loved her; I did, so much. I just loved Layla a whole lot more.

One morning, about a week before we were to visit family in N.Y. over Christmas, Sushi was having trouble breathing. The vet said she thought it was the beginning of the end. I had an unbearable decision to make. You know the one: for a few thousand dollars, I could extend her life another month or two, which meant leaving her in a strange cage in a strange place while I went to N.Y. with a heart full of guilt. Or…I could stay close and cancel our trip, in which case Layla would miss out on bonding with grandparents she rarely got to see. Or…there was that third option—*The Unthinkable Third Option*.

SUSHI HAD BEEN a great pet. Although she *could be* (and often *was)* unfriendly to my friends, she adored *me*. For sixteen years she slept on my pillow, and kissed my face with her rough little tongue. Personally, I'd rather have a pet that *doesn't* love everyone, because when they love only *you,* you know they really do. That's what made it so hard.

After a couple of sleepless nights, I made a painful decision. I woke up, put Layla and Sushi in the Jeep and headed for Sepulveda Animal Hospital. As I cradled my kitty in my arms, one-year-old Layla, upon discovering the colorful mural on the wall of the examining room, gleefully jumped up and down. "Cow say moooo, bird say tweeet," she squealed while my longtime companion, who had been with me through so much coming of age, was given an injection. Sushi's body went limp and they carried her away. *Sleep my sweet, sweet pet. I will miss you. I'm so sorry.*

When we were back in the Jeep, Layla pleaded for some Elmo. I hadn't the strength to deny her. I was crying uncontrollably but I knew that half the tears were from the relief I felt for being on the other side of *The Unthinkable Third Option*. Layla bopped up and down in that backseat with that mini box of raisins and that sippy cup: "La la la la, La la la la, Elmo's Song" filled the air. Oh, the juxtaposition.

Not long after that, as if the Universe wanted to make sure I was aware there were different levels of loss, the mom car and Adam's dad car (a Toyota Forerunner) were parked in the driveway and in the morning the Dad car was gone. Apparently, someone helped themselves to it along with all the contents (that handy Combi stroller, which fit perfectly and miraculously down an airplane aisle, Adam's golf clubs and a *Magical Mystery Tour* CD). Ugh! I think I was more upset about the CD than I was the stroller, or the golf clubs. But we didn't freak. It was just a car—a replaceable heap of metal. That's all. It didn't have a beating heart. It was small stuff. It really was.

As for 3-JIMMY-340, about a year after she was driven away, I received a letter in the mail from the adoptive parents expressing how much they loved her. How beautiful is *that*? Did you ever send anyone a thank-you note for something you bought from them on Craigslist or eBay? I was blown away. It was good to know someone was enjoying her even if it couldn't be me and that they hadn't crashed her into a tree. They were giving 3-JIMMY the love that I could no longer. I was overcome with closure.

It took a while but I had finally moved on and learned, to my surprise, there were things I *could* survive without—a city, a cat, a car, a father—and other things I almost denied myself, namely a true love and a child, that I came to cherish above all else.

Rest peacefully, Sushi.

Free Falling

OCCASIONALLY, ON A lucky day, I'm sitting at the Yamaha baby grand in my living room and a song falls from the sky and enters my body. This never happens when I'm waiting for it to happen. Hoping for it, willing it, or even thinking about it are deal breakers. It's sort of like chasing a nap. If I try too hard to fall asleep, I might as well forget about it. I have to let it sneak up on me. I have to give it (the song or the nap) the control. I have to have forgotten totally about the possibility of anything falling…for it to fall.

Almost Doesn't Count Almost Didn't

SUZAN KOÇ, MY new publishing point person at Hit & Run, was in a meeting with Craig Kallman at Atlantic Records discussing a Phil Collins tribute album. As the meeting was coming to a close, Suzan impulsively asked if she could play him a song. She tells me that the others in the room were annoyed because it had nothing to do with the matter at hand, but she didn't care. She played him the demo of my new song, "Almost Doesn't Count." As luck would have it, Craig thought it would be perfect for Brandy. I *loved* Brandy.

Looking back there are other things I love:

1. I love that Suzan had the nerve to fly by the seat of her pants.

2. I love that there was a time when an urban recording artist could sing a swagger-free song. Little did we know back then that someday soon it would become obligatory for just about everyone on Top 40 to adopt a hip hop attitude, whether he or she actually spoke with one or not.

3. I love that when Craig gave the song the thumbs-up, it was basically a done deal. Nowadays, there are so many considerations that come into play other than whether or not a song is exceptional, or a good fit for an artist. If this scenario were in a movie purporting to repre-

sent the current music business, it would be laughable. Even Craig would choke on his popcorn. (More on this topic later.)

I wasn't asked to come to the studio the day Guy, my co-writer, recorded Brandy's vocals. That was disappointing. Maybe he thought I'd steal some of the spotlight. I probably would have. Maybe he thought I'd want that photo-op. I probably would have. But so what? In any event, I didn't get to meet Brandy.

Soon after that, Guy got a call from Craig saying he wanted to recut the song (everything *but* the vocals) with a different producer. (I always wondered if that was karma for not having asked me to come by.) Craig felt the vibe should be more consistent with some other material they were recording. He wanted to give "Teddy J." (another producer who had been working with Brandy) a shot. Guy would still be getting production credit as they *were* going to keep the satin smooth, trademark Brandy vocals he recorded with her *the day I wasn't there.* I was happy about that, because that meant they were also keeping the background vocals that *I* subsequently sang (on a day *Brandy* wasn't there). You can hear me quite prominently on the record at the two-minute mark.

Guy and I crossed our fingers that Teddy J. wouldn't lose the essence of our song, but we agreed to reserve judgment until we heard his version. As it turned out, Teddy J. incorporated Latin flavored riffs and shimmers of bell trees. I've grown to appreciate this arrangement, but at the time we had what is known as *demo love:* this is when one gets so attached to a song in certain clothing that it's difficult to get used to it in a change of couture.

Drama ensued. A day before the album was to be mastered, we got a call from Teddy J.'s "Dadager" (Dad+manager) inquiring as to how much we'd be cutting Teddy J. in on the songwriting splits. *What?* Generally, if a third-party producer, who didn't participate in the writing of the song, is hired to take a record in a different direction, or slow down the tempo, or add bell trees, well…that's what a producer is paid to do. The church is separate from the state—*songwriting* and *producing.* I don't ask for a piece of a producer's fee. But the Dadager was adamant and said they wouldn't include it on the album if Teddy J. didn't get a piece of the songwriter's credit.

Does the Dadager have that power? If so, is he bluffing? Does Craig know about this? Do we even have time to investigate?

I recalled what had happened to "Live with Pride," the song I wrote for Wilson Phillips. That time I called their bluff and I lost. And, there was another issue: Let's say we gave Teddy J. a piece of "Almost Doesn't Count" and then, down the road, three other artists covered the song (re-recorded it for their own album) and sold a ton of records. Teddy J.'s name would be attached to those other versions as well, without ever having made a lyrical or melodic contribution and he would get a share of those royalties too.

This unabashed credit mongering was becoming an all-too-familiar industry practice. It was succeeding because so many writers were giving in. We didn't. (We also didn't sleep that night.) Fortunately, Brandy's album, *Never Say Never*, was mastered the next day with "Almost Doesn't Count" included. In all likelihood, today our song would be omitted without a second thought, replaced by another whose writers agreed to share the wealth. I can't say I wouldn't do the same. In certain situations, there's just *no* way around it anymore.

As it happened, the following year, Mark Wills recorded a splendid country rendition of "Almost" with producer Carson Chamberlain, who never asked to be cut in. The album reached RIAA certified Gold status in the U.S. I can't imagine how I would have felt if Teddy J.'s name were on that version, or if he had bought a new car with the royalties.

P.S. Despite all the drama and suspense that transpires between the birth of a song and its life as a record, the Universe still makes room for little miracles. On my birthday, while "Almost" (a single) was rising up the chart, I treated myself to a spa day at Burke Williams. As I stepped out of the shower buck naked, there was Brandy stepping out of the shower stall next to mine. (Thankfully, it wasn't Mark Wills.) Her skin was aglow and her hair was in a turban. It was an awkward place to be introducing myself (talk about boundaries), but I managed to find the nerve...and a towel. Still, no photo-op.

Snapshot: Maggie May

Here's how much I love "Maggie May": No matter where I am I can't listen to that song and not sing along—really loud. Crank it to 25. My daughter says, "Stop you're embarrassing me." I don't care. In the car is the best—top down…on the Ventura Freeway…hair blowing and annoyingly sticking to my lip gloss. What was wrong with Maggie? What on earth was she thinking? He loved her so much. She made a fool of him. First Class. She stole his heart. He wished he'd never seen her face. I'm exhilarated, nonetheless. Someone else's pain never made me feel so good.

So Sue Me (Twice)

BACK IN THE early '90s when I was still living in New York, hoping to work with writers who were more seasoned than I (because that's what ups your game), Gregg Sutton showed up at my 12th Street apartment with the devil in his eyes and a joint behind each ear. He was in town from L.A. on a writing trip. Molly Kaye, Gregg's publisher had set us up. She said she had a hunch.

Gregg's discography was serious. He had been on the road with Bob Dylan and had worked with Van Morrison. He was not only seasoned, he was out of my league, as far as I was concerned; fortunately Gregg didn't agree.

We did the *kiss-before-fucking* thing (i.e., took a long walk around the Village, smoked one of the joints, got some cappuccino), and *then* got to work. I found him fearless and uninhibited—raw and real. He wrought havoc on my orderly process, not to mention my tidy apartment. He was the teacher and I was student and I wanted to learn more.

So a few days later we reconvened in his dark smoky hotel room. Cross-legged on the floor, guitar in his arms, cigarette dangling from his lips, Gregg toggled back and forth between two chords and brazenly launched a random line: "Never before have I seen you look so blue." (Keep in mind this was 1990.) Now it was my turn. What could I add that would be as random, yet still relate? And there would be extra credit if it rhymed.

Don't think too much…go for it…just like he did:

"Can't find a cure and nothing comforts you?" He said nothing, but I could *feel* his approval.

Collaborating can be nerve-racking. A different co-writer might have balked at my line but a compatible partner can make you believe you were made for each other. Stylistically, Gregg and I were polar opposites—sweet and savory. But too much of the same thing is redundant—there's no contrast. So we *were* good together. Molly was right.

SHE SENT THE song we wrote that day, "Every Time You Cry," over to Clive Davis, who put it on hold. Back in 1993, if Clive Davis put your song "on hold," no matter how long he held it for (and that could be a long time), you didn't pitch it to any other artist. Occasionally Clive could *not* find a suitable home for your song. However, it was just as likely he would include it on something like *The Bodyguard* soundtrack (which sold 20 million copies) and you could buy yourself a *big fat house*. And a yacht. So we sat tight.

It took a while. In fact, it wasn't until I moved to the West Coast that Clive found an appropriate artist for "Every Time You Cry": Curtis Stigers, a blue-eyed soul singer, and saxophonist, who was coming off of a successful debut album. A number of renowned producers took a shot at cutting it with him, but Clive was not satisfied with the results. Gregg and I were getting antsy. We had passed up several opportunities for the song, fearing Clive's displeasure. So I did something unheard of for a mere songwriter, I asked Adam to take *my* matters into *his* hands and produce a version without Clive's knowledge or pre-approval, which meant Adam wouldn't be paid up front (or possibly ever) for anything. Then I got in touch with Curtis.

I thought there was a chance Curtis might be burnt out on the song. After all, he had recorded three versions already. On the contrary, *Curtis* thought there was a chance Clive wouldn't release his album until there was a production of which he approved. So Curtis met us at the studio and he sang it for the *fourth* time. We mixed it, put the DAT tape in a FedEx envelope and sent it to Clive. What did we have to lose?

The next day, a Monday, we were off to Cabo with our very good friends Kevin (REO) and Lisa (Speedwagon) Cronin for a week of R&R. The *next* day, Tuesday, I checked my answering machine and there was a message from Rose, Clive's secretary. She said that Clive loved Adam's version and wanted us to meet with him on Thursday at the Peninsula Hotel in Beverly Hills.

You have to understand…at the time that kind of good fortune happened to other people, not to us. (It was still a few years before *That Song*.) Now it seemed like the Universe was starting to make way. But since it had waited *this* long, couldn't it have waited one more week? Adam and I had just arrived in Cabo. To say the least, it was an inconvenient time for our luck to change. But this was Clive Davis. We packed our bags.

Thursday, at the Peninsula, Adam and I were greeted at the door of a penthouse suite and escorted to a living room where Clive was waiting in a large armchair. The room was equipped with a serious stereo system that clearly was not furnished by the hotel. Another A&R rep or two were present. More greetings. Clive knew who I was; as you may recall, Taylor Dayne was also an Arista artist. He was not one to forget a songwriter.

We got down to business; someone pressed "play." Adam and I couldn't take our eyes off of Clive—watching for any reaction or body language that might foreshadow the fate of our ambitious endeavor. Were we geniuses or were we fools? Such a fine line.

Clive's eyes were closed; his head nodding in rhythm with the song. You would have thought he'd never heard it before. When it was over, he seemed pleased, yet curious. He wanted to know how we got such an inspired vocal from Curtis. He was particularly impressed with what he referred to as, "the lilt." Adam and I exhaled. Whatever "the lilt" was we were fairly sure the fact that Clive was impressed with it meant he liked the rendition. The other A&R reps nodded and smiled in agreement; they liked it too.

The meeting was worth flying home for. The song was making it onto the record. Curtis would finally have his album released. Adam would get paid for a job he wasn't even hired to do (as opposed to the now all-too-common task of having to *beg* to get paid for a job you *were* hired to do).

Two days in Cabo with Adam,
Kevin (REO Speedwagon) and Lisa Wells-Cronin.

NOT LONG AFTER that, the publisher of "Take My Breath Away" (a huge hit performed by the band Berlin and featured in the 1986 film, *Top Gun*) heard "Every Time You Cry." It just so happened that the first five notes in the hook of "Every Time You Cry" were the same as the first five notes in the hook of "Take My Breath Away," and then they repeated. They repeated in "Take My Breath Away" too. Gregg and I sadly received correspondence saying they believed we had infringed on their song. Now that they mentioned it, there *was* a kind of a familiar ring to it. We must have been too caught up in *SongSex* on the day we wrote it to notice.

First we panicked. Then we consulted a musicologist who explained exactly what would constitute infringement:

1.   Similarity. Was there? Yes.

2.   Accessibility. Is it likely that the writers of the alleged infringing song (Shelly and Gregg) had previously heard the earlier work?

Umm…"Take My Breath Away" was a *ginormous* hit. We heard it a lot. Yes. Yes. Definitely.

3. The issue of "Prior Art." *Was* there material that pre-dated "Take My Breath Away" that contained the same sequence of notes? Yes. In fact, the musicologist found that the melody in question was a diatonic motif that had been around for hundreds of years, far before pop music ever popped—loads of "Prior Art." There was no infringement because "Take Me Breath Away" wasn't as original as its publisher thought it was. The case disappeared—another *huge* sigh of relief.

Alas, upon the release of Curtis's album, Curtis, being candid and off the cuff, apparently said something in an interview that did not sit well with the label. The album was released, but it didn't get much promotion and that was that. All that effort; such a short life. Poof—easy come, easy go.

A few years later and seventy-five hundred miles away, Australia's John Farnham recorded "Every Time You Cry" as a duet with the vocal group, Human Nature. Easy go, easy come. The song went to No. 1. Not too shabby at all.

P.S. Adam and I have become quite fond of the word "lilt" and often refer to it when we hear a song we particularly like.

No. 1

IT WAS THE last week of the twentieth century. Everyone was in disbelief that it was coming to a close, and Y2K mania was everywhere. I was cuddled up with two-year-old Layla at bedtime reading *Winnie the Pooh*. She smelled of baby shampoo and Mustela. This part of the day was sacred. The cordless phone happened to be by my side only because I had just gotten off of a call.

"What a Girl Wants" was No. 11 on the *Billboard* Hot 100 singles chart. In 1999, the *Billboard* Hot 100 was the Holy Grail—*the* chart that mattered. I was familiar with No. 2 on the Hot 100. "Bitch" had reached No. 2 in 1997, when I was pregnant.

That "Bitch" never made it to No. 1 was a humbling yet character-building experience for me. It was kept out of the top slot by Puff Daddy (aka Sean John Combs, P. Diddy, Diddy, *Puffy*—you know the guy) and his cover version of "Every Breath You Take" (aka "I'll Be Watching You"), a tribute to Biggie Smalls (aka The Notorious B.I.G.), the rapper who was gunned down in a drive-by shooting during a long East Coast/West Coast hip-hop feud. How do you compete with *that*? I decided this was the Universe's way of telling me that my child was going to take over the No. 1 position in my life, and songs—they would be my children as well, but they would have to take a back seat.

Still, a girl wants what she wants, and what this girl wanted was a No. 1 song…on the Hot 100. She wanted it bad. But she had a toddler to care for, feed, bathe, take to the park, pick up, put down, pick up again, put down—you get the picture. She was busy, and she didn't have as much time to ponder possibilities as she used to.

The phone rang. I glanced at the incoming number and saw that it was Pete Ganbarg, an A&R exec who had worked on the Santana record that was out at the time, *Supernatural*…the one on which there was a guest pop star on every track, singing along with Carlos's guitar. One of those songs, a collaboration with Matchbox 20 heartthrob Rob Thomas, called "Smooth," had been No. 1 for six weeks. That's a long time.

What does Pete want? I like Pete. Sometimes he asks me to write with one of his artists. But, sometimes he asks ten other writers to do the same thing, so the chances of MY song getting the *love are severely diminished. And besides, when he asks so many writers, a girl just doesn't feel special. So, do I want to take this call?*

Pooh was just about to stick his paw in the *hunny* pot and Layla was waiting for me to turn the page, when I did a very bad thing—I answered the phone. Pete couldn't hold back. He skipped the small talk.

"I wanted to tell you 'What a Girl Wants' is going to knock out 'Smooth' next week. You're going to have the first No. 1 song of the Millennium!"

"Shut *up!*" I thought.

"Shut *up!*" I said. But Pete swore it was true.

Now this is the music business. Ninety-five percent of the stuff people swear is true turns out to be false. Not because they mean to deceive you, but because there are so many variables and usually one of them gets in the way. I didn't know whether to totally freak out or take it with a grain of salt and feign elation. Just to be on the safe side, I chose the latter. To get invested in the idea of a No. 1 on the Hot 100 could be imprudent and devastating should it not happen.

However, the feigning didn't last very long. I got off the phone, finished reading *Pooh*, tucked the covers around my baby, took a deep whiff of her, kissed her delicious *keppe*, turned down the light and sat in the rocker for what seemed like eternity until she was definitely, without a doubt, positively sleeping. I tiptoed out of the room and shut the door ever so gently behind me. And then…I did one of those silent screams while jumping up and down pogo stick style in the hallway.

As it turned out, Pete was right. When I opened *Billboard* the following week "What a Girl Wants" was in the No. 1 position on the Hot 100 and there was an "S. Peiken" (and a "G. Roche") by its side. Pete will always have a special place in my heart for delivering such outstanding news. To this day, every time I hear "Every Breath You Take" aka "I'll Be Watching You," I cringe. When I hear "Smooth," I smile. And when I contemplate the logic as to why "Bitch" never made it all the way and "What a Girl Wants" did, I believe that the Universe rewarded me with a No.1 because I had let go of the expectation.

Claude Mitchell, Suzan Koç, Guy Roche, Christina Aguilera,
Me, Steven Rosen (Guy's manager), Ron Fair…
backstage at the Universal Amphitheater where
Christina was opening for TLC.

I Could Cry

AFTER MY VERY brief first marriage to Russell had ended, I was the happiest girl in the world to be free, but it had been a heart-wrenching ride. From the moment we met until the day we parted, I'd been on a rollercoaster of excitement, anticipation, doubt, confusion, love, resentment, regret, disappointment, and relief. I was emotionally exhausted. There were no tears left, but there *were* words:

> *I can't cry,*
> *Though my tears would fill an ocean.*
> *I can't cry like I did before.*
> *Can't deny*
> *This heart's still badly broken,*
> *But I can't cry no more.*

In 1988, I could write a song about *my* personal life and still have a good shot at finding someone to sing it. Not every artist was interested in writer's credit. If the song resonated with them in a meaningful way, they would record it.

I had developed a relationship with Ric Wake (producer of "Carry Your Heart"). He had become a fan of my work and occasionally was instrumental in getting a song to a recording artist who I couldn't access myself.

He had an "in" with Natalie Cole. We crossed our fingers. Natalie liked the song. It was a go.

These days, because we're often writing *with* pop stars we hang out in the studio together, order in lunch, go out for a coffee, tweet some selfies. By the time we're ready to record vocals, we're already quite acquainted. But back then, there was a bit more reverence and distance between *us* and *them*. If you weren't producing (which I wasn't), you were rarely present when a major artist recorded your song. So I never got to meet Natalie Cole when she recorded "I Can't Cry." I would have loved to. I would have loved to have thanked her for singing my song.

Not long after I transplanted from N.Y. to L.A., I was in a salon getting my hair cut and there, *snip snip*, in the mirror in front of me, *snip snip*, was the reflection of a very familiar face getting *her* hair done as well. Is that? Umm…not sure…reading a magazine…is it? *Snip snip*…Yup, that's her. Natalie Cole. Here we go again…like Carly in the elevator…to approach or not to approach? Where is it acceptable and what are the boundaries?

Once, I was on a plane with a very young Layla and an Olsen Twin was sitting near us. I don't know which one it was. They look exactly the same to me. Layla wanted to approach. I explained, "Not on a plane, honey, because if the Olsen twin wants to extract herself from the situation, she can't. But as soon as the doors open, go for it." When we landed, Layla followed that Olsen Twin down the ramp and into a Starbucks where she got a signature on a napkin. Good girl—both of them.

Having said that, the urge to approach Natalie Cole was acute. I hadn't been in the room when she gave birth to my song. I wasn't beside her telling her to breathe, to push. I wasn't even watching quietly from behind a pane of glass. I was simply not part of the experience at all. Bonding with her now, even ever so briefly, would give me the thrill I had been denied.

Furthermore, I wanted her to know:

I am important. There is a story behind that song. The song came from someone! And that…that someone is me—the girl in the chair a few feet away from you. We are breathing the same air. What are the chances? If you knew I was so close, surely you would want to hug me. Okay…at least cordially shake my hand and be happy to meet me. Wouldn't you?

So it wasn't just about me thanking Natalie Cole (although I definitely wanted to). It was about *her* thanking *me*. I had to seize this opportunity to let her know who I was, so that she could. For then, my talent would be acknowledged…my *raison d'être* validated.

Snip snip…our respective hairdressers swiveled our chairs around and Natalie Cole and I were face to face. I couldn't take it anymore. I shimmied out of my seat and I did it—I approached.

"Excuse me, Miss Cole, I'm Shelly Peiken." Awkward pause. "You recorded a song of mine a few years ago." I extended my hand.

Without moving her head, she raised her eyes from her magazine. I was standing looking down at her. She was sitting looking up at me. She wasn't smiling. I retracted my hand. I regretted it immediately. It's hard enough to be intruded upon when you're camera ready…but trapped in a chair with all that stinky goo in your hair and foil on your head? And the dishwater gray smock? Nobody really wants to be seen that way. Nobody wants to chat. I should have known better; I *did* know better. I didn't need to give thanks. I didn't really need to get any. But it was too late.

Fortunately, Natalie Cole was gracious.

"Oh? What song was that?" she inquired.

Now, you can plan it out all you want, exactly what you're going to say to someone. Tell yourself to keep it simple. The thing is, you just don't know what's going to come out when you open your mouth, because adrenaline changes *everything*.

"I Can't Cry"? I posed it as a question, as if I wasn't sure of the answer. And to give her some wiggle room in case she didn't remember it.

"Oh," she replied warmly. "Of course!"

I should have left it at that—short and sweet. Quit while I was ahead… grateful for eye contact and the brief meet and greet. Deep down? I knew who I was. I didn't need reassurance. I should have just said, "Well *so* nice to meet you, Miss Cole…sorry to disturb." Instead, I spewed some verbal diarrhea.

"Yes, well, it was about my *divorce!* And how painful it was and how I actually *couldn't* cry any more…Are *you dee-vorced?*" It was too much TMI.

I knew it as soon as it came out of my mouth. She sensed my mortification and that made her uncomfortable and she cut straight to…

"Well, very nice to meet you, Shelly." She swiveled her chair back around and continued reading her magazine. I didn't blame her. I skipped the blow dry—couldn't get out of there fast enough.

Layla following an Olsen twin off the plane.

Come On Over, Shelly

SOMETIMES OPPORTUNITIES KNOCK in inconvenient places. Open the door wherever you are.

The bathroom was steaming up. I was tucking my hair into a polka dot shower cap when the phone rang. It was Ron Fair. He told me that "Come on over, Baby (All I Want Is You)" was going to be Christina's next single. He felt confident about this choice. Only thing was, he thought the lyrics on the verses could be stronger.

Thank you for sharing, Ron. But what does that have to do with me? I didn't write "Come on over, Baby."

This was true but he wanted me to have a go at tightening up the lyrics anyway.

Okay, but the album is out already. There's nothing you can do about it now…is there?

Indeed there was. Ron said Christina could re-sing the song and the label could service the alternate version to radio.

Really? Wow. I've never heard of such a thing. I know that sometimes I'm a little out of the loop, but okay. *I'm not going to argue. I'd love to be the one who tightens up that lyric.*

I will always have occasional struggles with confidence. I can convince myself I merely get lucky from time to time. This is why I was grateful that Ron called *me* because that meant *he* thought I knew what I was doing. Once, I heard Ron describe me as "the bomb" (when it was cool to *be* the bomb). That made me feel great. Not long after that I overheard him describe Anne ("Torn") Preven as the bomb. This made me realize that there are a lot of bombs all over this town. And he might have called a few already, but he called me too. So I'd better get moving.

First I wanted to make sure the original writers were aware Ron was asking me to do this. If you're going to mess with someone else's original creation, it's only right to get their blessing. He confirmed that they knew.

I'd like to tell you I was in no rush…that I showered, checked my email, called my mother, put on some pasta water and then got started. But it didn't happen like that.

Here's how it did: as soon as we got off the phone, and while the bathroom steamed up and the mirrors got foggier, I loaded up the CD player next to the sink and with nothing on but that polka dot shower cap, I tried out an assortment of words and phrases over the existing ones and scratched out possibilities on the cardboard packaging attached to a new batch of plastic razors. And *then* I took a shower. *Then* I checked my email. And *then* I put on some pasta water and *then* called my mother.

A FEW MONTHS later the "Come on over, Baby" that you heard on the radio had completely different verses than the one on the album. *My* verses. It wasn't your imagination *in case* you had the album and *in case* you were paying attention and *in case* you care. (I have to assume you care because you're reading this book.)

And I had another No. 1 record to my credit, thanks again, Ron Fair. When someone asks me if I wrote "Come on Over" I feel it's my duty to explain that I didn't birth that baby. I wasn't in the room when it was conceived, but I foster-parented it to some extent.

Would it have been a hit without the re-write? Maybe. Ron would probably say no. I would hope he'd be right.

Breaking Away

I USED TO venture out on international writing trips—London, Germany, Sweden. A change in scenery, architecture, and terrain can do a creative person a lot of good. Travel expands the mind no matter what or where or why, and no matter how the songs turned out, a trip was always a rewarding adventure. It was also important for my publisher to see I could mobilize should an overseas opportunity arise.

But that was all "B.C." Before Child. "A.C.," that maternal pull that had me thinking twice about leaving...*truly* had me thinking twice about leaving. Not that Adam couldn't hold down the fort, but, well, it was just easier when *I* was there. At least *I* thought so. *I* was the one arranging play dates and making PBJs. There would be a lot of pre-arranging to do if *I* were to leave...and finger-crossing that everything would come off without a hitch. It was possible *everything* would fall apart.

At the same time, I thought it was healthy for my child to see I had a passion...to be aware that having a career and being her mother were not mutually exclusive. It was essential I remind *myself* of that *too* once in a while. So occasionally, even after thinking twice about leaving, or three times or four, I would go. And if Suzan (now my good friend as well as my publisher) were free to come with, even better. When Layla was in first grade, Suzan and I went on one of those trips.

When we got to the hotel in London, I called home to let Adam know I arrived safely. He said Layla wanted to talk to me. She got on the phone and sounded very excited to deliver some news.

"Guess what, Mama?" she said.

"What, baby, tell me, tell me."

"I have head lice." I was not twelve hours out the door.

"That's wonderful, honey. Put Daddy back on the phone."

Adam pulled it together and did all the necessary tasks. He stripped the beds, boiled the linens and trucked Layla down to Hair Genies (a salon that removes the lice *and* makes it fun at the same time!). For a few hundred bucks, they diligently combed through her tangled locks looking for nits and stressed how important it was to bring her back the next day for another hundred bucks.

While Adam was stripping and boiling and trucking, I pondered the idea of women having it all. How *much* is all? What *is* all anyway? Sometimes I think the women who swear they have whatever all *is* are either lying, denying, or somewhere a child is missing their mommy. But Adam and Layla did just fine. They survived, *and* thrived. So maybe it was the Mommy missing the child. Either way, it's a tricky balance. For me (the woman who wasn't sure she wanted a child), the umbilical cord was never completely severed.

P.S. Adam and I always wondered about those head lice. The technicians at "Hair Genies" never actually presented a nit. Perhaps they sponsored the nurse who went to the school to do the random check and it wouldn't be so good for business if lice were not detected on somebody somewhere. I dunno. Juss sayin'.

P.P.S. Having Suzan with me on international writing trips was a blessing for reasons other than companionship. AC (After Child), my head was never as clear when I traveled because a piece of my mind was always at home. She helped me stay focused, reminded me of where I was going and who would be there when I arrived. She got me international cell phones, made sure I got on the correct tube (underground transportation), and sometimes even packed me a lunch.

Thinking twice about leaving.

Napster

IF A TREE falls in a forest and no one is around to hear it, does it make a sound? Of course it does. By the same token, if you can listen to a song but can't touch the medium on which it is delivered, is it still someone's intellectual property? Should you still have to pay for it now that it arrives via an invisible digital transfer? Or, should you get it for free simply because you can?

Something happened at the tail end of the twentieth century that took the music business by surprise, calling into question the way we, as a society, value music. Napster, an online file-sharing service, reared its ugly head and made it possible to download music without paying for it. (It was as if people were walking into the Gap and stealing the jeans.) This spawned a new generation that assumed music was free. Some said this was justifiable karma because they felt they'd been over paying for music for quite some time. Perhaps. But songwriters' livelihoods would become severely compromised in the process.

Basking in the glow of my recent successes, I wasn't paying a lot of attention. Why concern myself with such unpleasantries? Napster wasn't here to stay; surely *some*one would do *some*thing. But, it turned out to have a much bigger and more lasting impact than anyone could have imagined.

By 2002, "digital piracy" had caused a deadly drop in record sales worldwide. Right around that time, I did a phone interview and was asked if I knew how much income I had lost from online file sharing for "What a Girl Wants" alone. I hadn't done the math. But when I got off the call, I did. And I realized what a fog I'd been in.

Lawsuits were filed and Napster was shut down, but like a game of whack-a-mole, a wide variety of alternative services replaced it. By the time the industry came to the realization that it had to embrace technology, work *with* these services, and find a way to evolve, it was too late. Record stores were already closing, labels shrinking and jobs disappearing. The music business would never be the same.

Suzan, My Wife

I MET SUZAN in 1995 when she was working for Warner/Chappell Music in Paris. She and her boss Jean Davoust were in Los Angeles on business and they wanted to present me with a plaque for "Sensualite," a song I had written with their writer, Albert ("It Never Rains in Southern California") Hammond, which had reached Gold status in France. I thought that was very nice of Suzan and Jean. I have never said no to a Gold plaque. We met for drinks on the rooftop of Le Park Hotel. She made the presentation, we took some photos, and then she returned to Paris.

Little did I know what a force Suzan would become in my life. I'm sure she had no idea either. In 1996, I was going on my fifth year as a writer with Hit & Run Music. They were small, but they were smart. They saw the big picture. They signed that Right Said Fred song, "I'm Too Sexy" when nobody else would touch it. And they were savvy enough to poach Suzan from Warner/Chappell Music and move her from Paris to N.Y. Fortunately for me, after a year they continued moving her west, this time from N.Y. to L.A. There we were again. Face to face. I had just had a baby and I needed *help!* It was as if the Universe sent me a Fairy God-Sister.

From working day in and day out with Suzan, I learned how valuable a passionate and dedicated publisher could be. She paid attention. She listened to every song. She had some strong opinions, but thankfully she *had* some. She told me when a song was special. She told me when it wasn't. She'd bust me for the one mediocre line in the middle that, come to think of it, never felt right in the first place. She'd arrange collaborations with co-writers whose strengths were my weaknesses. There were other publishers who did what she did. But she did it better. She was like the Songwriter Whisperer. Just not as quiet.

On Jan 1, 2000, the day "What a Girl Wants" reached No. 1, little Hit & Run was sold to one of the major publishing giants. How's that for a high and a low in one day? I went from being one of six writers at a boutique company to one of hundreds. Suzan took a job with another publishing company with the understanding that she would still look after me on the side. It was a minor conflict of interest that everyone could live with. (Compared to the conflicts of interests in the music business today, it was a blip. But I'm getting ahead of myself.) By this time, we were spending more and more time together. We became each other's confidants, plus-ones, sidekicks, wing-women, co-conspirators.

During the summer of 2001, while en route to Europe, Suzan developed a frightening headache, which turned out to be a brain aneurism. The friend she was traveling with called to tell me she was in surgery in Boston and that *hopefully everything would be all right.* This was surreal and serious. A lot of people didn't survive brain aneurisms. I got on a plane for Boston.

The chief of neurology was on call that night, which might have been the factor that saved Suzan's life. She came through. The biggest complication was an unsightly scar on her hairline. So what.

We were pretty much inseparable after that.

A few years ago I asked Adam for an opinion: the black jeans or the white. He chose the white. My response? "Are you sure? Don't they make my butt look flat?" To which he replied, "Why don't you just ask your *wife?*" I knew exactly who he was talking about. And from that moment on, that's who Suzan was. It made perfect sense. She was one of my best friends; she'd take me to airports and pick me up from the doctor. She adored my daughter. She knew how to load my dishwasher. We vacationed effortlessly. She didn't hear me snore. My wife—it's nice to have one.

As the economic landscape of the music industry grew more challenging, publishing companies had to downsize. Suzan became a free agent, as did hundreds of other seasoned "creatives." I understand why these companies had to tighten their belts, and maybe they didn't have a choice, but in the process they were dismissing invaluable resources…losing sight of that big picture…hiring younger, sexier, more affordable novices to fill the shoes of experienced song whisperers. Collaborations were arranged without considering compatibility. Songs were pitched randomly with the thought being if enough spaghetti was thrown up against the wall something would stick. It became quantity before quality—acquisition before passion.

Suzan is anything but idle. However, the day-to-day mentorship that I was so lucky to have received, publisher to writer, is becoming a thing of the past. Writers can grow on their own, but not as many will thrive without someone who will lift them up when they're too hard on themselves, or tell them the truth—even when they don't want to hear it. And that's a pity, because that's what makes us better.

The Mother App Revisited

LOOKING BACK ON my reasons to remain childish…I mean child*less*, I have since had the following re-evaluations: *See below in italics.*

1. If I had a baby I'd have to grow up.
   Oh grow up!

2. If I grew up, I'd be closer to my death.
   When your time is up, your time is up.

3. Pregnancy leads to stretch marks and saggy boobs.
   I invested in support bras and Spanx. Victoria told me the secret.

4. I'd be kowtowing to cultural expectations, as well as pressure from my mother, sister, and girlfriend, Lucy.
   I had a baby because I wanted to have a baby, not because they wanted me to.

5. I'd gain weight.
   I did. I lost some, not all of it. It's fine.

6. I would no longer be on call for the ebb and flow of creative musings.
   Inevitably, I lost some clever ideas. I found others I never would have found if life hadn't gotten "bigger."

7. What if I left my baby at the mall?
   That never happened. Not even close.

8. I'd lose my edge and start writing lullabies.
   I wrote one lullaby.

9. I'd have to give up my Miata.
   That was a bummer.

10. Having that much more to love means having that much more to lose.
    That's true. It's terrifying.

My own mother passed away from complications due to Parkinson's disease in 2003. I've heard that, on the average, a retired senior lives about eight years after losing a spouse. That's exactly how much longer she lived after my father died. She was a devoted and loving mother. Sometimes I thought she loved me too much. It wasn't until I was a mother myself that I realized there is just no such thing.

My Mom, Sydelle Peiken.

Map to My Song

I GOT SOME good news from Guy. He had pitched our song, "Map to My Heart" to Vito Luprano, Celine Dion's A&R man, and Vito called to say Celine wanted to cut it. This being the fourth song of mine she would record, I thought it was high time to introduce myself. Despite the Natalie Cole debacle, I still had this hope that a singer would welcome the chance to express appreciation for the unsung hero: the songwriter who had written the words and melodies she would soon be making her own!

Suzan urged me to call Vito and invite myself to Vegas where Celine was working on a new album. Suzan was wise. I called. I told Vito I was going to be in Vegas the following weekend for a wedding (a fib), and that if Celine was going to be recording (I knew she was), I'd love to stop by (with Suzan; I was not going to do this alone). He told me it would be fine, although it wasn't *my* song she'd be recording that day. (This I knew, but I didn't care. I just wanted to meet Celine.)

Suzan and I prepared for an adventure: Vegas—land of neon and over-stimulation—at a time in my life when I was becoming more interested in finding my zen. We snuck some caviar and toast points through security for a little snack en route.

When we landed in Sin City, we thought we saw a record producer we knew walking through the terminal. "Jeff Spiker" used to be my friend.

Adam and I were very close with him and his wife, "Shaylene," along with another couple, "Rich" (another fellow producer), and "Darcy."

A little back story is required here: When I first moved to L.A., Rich and I became fast friends. He introduced me to the very talented but somewhat shy, Jeff, who was just returning to the business after taking a break due to some personal matters. Rich was helping Jeff re-acclimate. He turned him on to fresh faces, engineers and Auto-Tune experts, singers and musicians. Jeff, Rich and I began working together. We were all waiting for our big break. Even a small one would have been sufficient. It was a jungle out there. We were rooting for each other. Life started getting back to normal for Jeff; he was becoming less and less shy every day. That's when our families got closer—barbecues, vacations, birthday cakes.

As luck would have it, Rich was asked by a record label if he would spend some time developing a promising artist they were considering signing. Assuming all went well, Rich would produce her album. It looked like this might finally be *his* big break. Then one day Rich went to the studio and found *Jeff* producing the same girl in a room down the hall. Before he knew it, Jeff was producing the entire record. Rich said Jeff never called him, or bothered to walk down the hall to tell him to his face. He found out from the label. Not surprisingly, that was the end of their friendship.

The artist in question blew up and suddenly Jeff's name was on the tip of everyone's tongue and on the top of every list, including the Grammy nominations. He got very busy and I wasn't working with him as often, but that was okay. He would still call if he were writing with an artist who needed a lyric buddy. A year or so later, however, he somehow *overlooked* my contribution (albeit a small one) to a song we had written with the latest "it-girl" he was producing. When my name wasn't listed on the label copy, I noticed and called him on it. He made the correction, but sadly, that was more or less the end of our relationship as well.

So although it was conceivable that Jeff *was* in Vegas producing Celine Dion, Suzan and I really wanted it *not* to be him, as it would surely put a damper on things. We proceeded to our hotel, where we had dinner and martinis. Then we called Vito who gave us the secret password to give to the Palms Casino security guard who would allow us into the elevator that would take us to the private floor where Celine was recording. *What an unlikely place for a studio.* The elevator doors opened to a dark hallway.

There was some light coming from the crack of a door so we took a chance and knocked. A young woman answered and offered us a seat in a waiting area. Soon, Vito came to fetch us and led us into a dimly lit control room where René (Celine's husband) was listening quietly with some friends. Suzan and I nodded respectfully and took a seat. We whispered a bit. There was Celine behind the glass, singing. She sounded amazing! She sounded just like Celine! Very exciting indeed, except…I couldn't help but notice a familiar baseball cap atop a familiar silhouette behind the mixing console.

Jeff Spiker swiveled around in his chair and there was an awkward silence as I came into focus. He faked "happy" to see me. I faked it back. Suzan did some faking. We made (very) small talk. He swiveled back around.

Celine looked frustrated, like she was having trouble connecting with the song. She removed her headphones and laid them on the music stand. Everybody held their breath waiting to see if she was going to call it a night. It appeared she was. She walked away from the mic and came into the lounge outside the control room.

Uh, oh. This was a development I had not planned for—Celine Dion in a foul mood. Still, I had come all this way with a mission. I wasn't going to let Jeff Spiker, or a foul mood, throw me off track. Actually, I had forgotten all about Jeff Spiker as I inched my way toward Celine. And when I was close enough I said,

"Celine? I mean Miss Dion? I mean, Celine?"

I heard myself thinking:

Careful. Remember what happened with Natalie. Don't spew. Keep it short. Tell her who you are—The Unsung Hero! Give her a chance to compose herself and express appreciation.

But it didn't matter what I was *thinking*, because as soon as I had her attention, that adrenaline kicked in again. I lost the plot and launched into the names of all the songs of mine that she'd recorded ("SupaLove," "If I

Were You," "Forget Me Not"). I simply couldn't think of anything else to say.

I'm sure Celine didn't know what the hell I was babbling on about. In all fairness, her head was probably still in the song she'd just abandoned. It was obvious she didn't take it lightly. She *was* trying to be polite but in her confusion, she muttered something like, "Uh," and that was enough for me. If she was *going* to express appreciation, I'll never know, because I said, "So nice to meet you," and Suzan and I headed for the door.

You can't force a moment. The best ones happen all by themselves. Clearly, one was not happening here. But looking through that glass witnessing Celine Dion bring a song to life with her golden voice, knowing that the following week she'd be doing the same with one of mine (hopefully with better results), in this case, was a moment in itself. The trip had been worth it.

When I got back to L.A., I decided to call Jeff—if just to find some humor in the elephant that had been in that control room. Perhaps forgiveness could be mustered from both of us; deep down I wondered if I had judged him too harshly. Maybe I was only seeing what had transpired over those last few years from one perspective—Rich's. After all, this was someone who was once my friend…someone I cared about—someone I laughed with—commiserated with. Maybe we could clear the air. But the conversation was forced, and he made sure to let me know that the song Celine had walked out on was one he wrote, and because Suzan and I distracted her, he had lost the cut.

Wow. What a blamer! Celine couldn't hear anything behind that sound-proof glass and it was so dark, I'm sure she couldn't see us.

I had let my guard down and he shot that puck right past me. It must have made him feel better to believe it was somebody else's fault.

One week later Celine recorded "Map to My Heart." Jeff wasn't producing. And sadly, I wasn't there. There might have been a few *other* people whispering behind the glass, but if there were, it didn't bother Celine, because she included the song on her album.

Snapshot: Time Travel

Classic hits beam me back to my youth, the loss of which, if you haven't figured it out by now, I have not recovered from fully. I hear "The Joker" or "Come and Get Your Love" and I enter a portal and I land hard there where I heard it the first time…at that party…making out with that football player…intoxicated from Heaven Scent and Aramis and Strawberry Hill, blinded by the blissful ignorance (or was it innocence?) that had me believing the delirium was going to last forever. Everything was sublime. For three minutes, I was back at that party and it was a wonderful visit.

Cirque du Beatles

WHEN LAYLA WAS eleven years old, our family of three "Southwested" over to Las Vegas to see Cirque du Soleil's *LOVE*. I had always enjoyed Cirque shows in the past…the choreography, the acrobatics, the whole visual extravaganza…but I wouldn't have gone so far out of my way to see another, especially to Vegas—you know how I feel about Vegas and all that neon. The theme of *this* show, however, was Beatles, and that changed things. I had been telling Adam that we'd better get up there before the show moved on, because missing it would definitely have made me cranky.

One of the obsessions that Adam and I have shared over the years is our insatiable hunger for all things Beatles. Driving across Mulholland in the Hollywood Hills, if a playlist shuffles to *Rubber Soul,* we revel in the discovery of a harmony we never noticed before and the discussion commences. We analyze the Dylanesque-ness of "You've Got to Hide Your Love Away." Are we "a John" or are we "a Paul"? Who really *carried that weight*? How incredible it was that their stars collided and they actually found each other? What were the chances? How lucky for them. How lucky for us. This is the way it has always been for Adam and me…an ongoing never-ending exchange of which we never tire.

Now we have a kid in the backseat, chiming in. I am proud to say Layla is as fanatical about the Beatles as her parents. I often wonder whether there is a recessive Beatles gene, because if there is, she must have inherited it along with the color of her eyes—our own little Fab Four connoisseur. To have her knowledgeably participate in this dialogue is poetic, joyous, adorable, hysterical and scary. We love it.

I was a small child when I fell. At the first sight of those skinny pants and dangling cigarettes, all I wanted to do was get close enough to smell them, to hold their hand, close my eyes and let them kiss me (on the cheek)…or tell me a secret. That's about as intimate as my fantasies got.

Layla might not have "been there," but I believe she "goes there" retroactively. There's a poster of *Abbey Road* over her closet to which she wakes up every morning. She has buttons and coasters and T-shirts and playing cards. She listens to "For No One" when she brushes her teeth and plays "If I Fell" on the piano. And she knows what I mean when I tell her "Across the Universe" is an out-of-body experience.

The Beatles pulled us into a place we didn't know existed—a world of uncontrived, uncalculated delicious madness…of minor to major to minor again, of dropped measures and bizarre segues. Yet, the absence of logic never made so much sense. Anything was possible. They cooked with spices we never tasted. It was like we were all virgins and we shall never get that flower back. I miss them. I miss something having that much power over me.

LOVE was mind-blowing. The theatrics artfully chronicled and interpreted the Beatles' story, while a killer soundtrack of medleys and mash-ups radiated from speakers in the headrest of every seat in the house. It was like one big Sgt. Pepper's hallucination without the LSD. I wanted it to go on and I certainly could have sat through it twice. It was totally worth the exposure to all the neon.

When it was over, I saw a frizzy haired middle-aged woman mouthing the words and bobbing her head to "Lady Madonna" as the song ushered the crowd out of the theatre. Suddenly, I felt territorial and possessive. Who was this strange woman singing the words that were so familiar to me? How could she possibly comprehend my personal collision and how deep it cut. Then I reconsidered. Maybe I had it all wrong and anyone who ever fell feels exactly the same, even, perhaps, my daughter.

6 Degrees of John Lennon

ON A LONDON writing trip in the mid '90s, I was asked if I'd be interested in working with Julian Lennon. We were both signed to Hit & Run Music at the time, and Michelle de Vries, who worked for the company in the U.K., was our mutual friend. Julian didn't go on too many songwriting blind dates because apparently a lot of writers wanted to work with him simply because of who he was. She assured him I wasn't one of those people...but...well...I sort of was. I mean, there are celebrities and there are Beatles, and to me it's apples and oranges. You could put me in a room with George Clooney and I wouldn't flinch. Julian was different; he would be the closest I'd ever come (in spirit) to John. Of course, I said, "yes."

In all fairness to me, I had always liked his music. I bought *Valotte,* and Julian's fourth album, *Help Yourself,* with the song "Saltwater," long before this writing opportunity arose. I never would have been *as* enthusiastic, if I wasn't a true fan. I promise.

Michelle arranged for us to meet at Julian's South Kensington flat. Here are some things I remember:

- The flat was carpeted from wall to wall in white (just like pictures I had seen of John and Yoko's apartment in the Dakota). Lavender incense filled the air.

- While writing, Julian made reference to "a father" as it applied to the song we were writing…and it was bizarre because, well, you know why.

- His mother phoned…that would be Cynthia…as in Cynthia Lennon. (Rest peacefully, Cynthia.) And I heard him talking to her. I remembered her from the teen magazine, *Tiger Beat!* She had bangs and a flip. They never wanted to tell anyone John was married. I don't know how they thought they could keep it a secret.

- When we recorded our song, "Take Time," Julian sounded eerily like John, especially when I closed my eyes, and squeezed them really tight.

- Julian was going out of town and offered his flat to me for the remainder of my stay. I accepted. I used his shower and I slept in his bed. And…I came across a photograph of him and John on a bureau…a personal artifact that perhaps had never been published. I felt a little voyeuristic, but it's not like I opened a drawer or peeked in a closet.

- On my last night, I had a dream that Julian and I had a baby—a Beatles grandchild. Paul was Godfather, and he wrote a song for the baby called "Hey Lil' Jude." I woke up feeling very silly.

In all seriousness, Julian was a soft-spoken and talented artist for whom I would have had affection, no matter who his father was. It was just *so* hard to ignore who his father was.

P.S. While in London Julian and I had gone to a pub with some other writer friends and one of them had taken a picture of us. I kept it in a safe place for years but, mysteriously, I haven't been able to find it. It serves me right because I proclaimed to be so nonplussed by it all. And I guess that was a bit of a non-truth. I was definitely "plussed." But, a few days after writing this (and years after last seeing him), quite remarkably and coincidentally (I swear), I ran into Julian at the Sunset Marquis. He was in town briefly and invited me to a party that evening where his photography would be on display in their new gallery. On the way, I picked up Suzan. It was a zoo, but we found him. She took this photo and I made up for something I lost.

Snapshot: Across the Universe

People always ask me what my favorite Beatles
song is. I look at them like they are nuts. How
on earth can you pick *just one Beatles song?* But,
I've changed my mind. I *have* a favorite and it is
"Across the Universe." Final Answer. The irony
is, I can barely listen to it because it hurts too
much. I want to tell you in detail why this is so,
but I can't. It just does. There's no better language
than the song itself. I'm not sure even John knew
what he was talking about when his words were
flowing into a paper cup. But it doesn't matter. The
sound of it breaks my heart. That's what counts.
Perhaps the best thing a song can do is *make*
us feel something, even if it makes no sense.

Eargasms

I'M ON THE treadmill listening to JackFM on my radio headset. (I like listening to the radio because there's an element of surprise that I don't get when I'm listening to a self-programmed playlist.) JackFM strings together ten song snippets of classics: a teaser of what I might hear at any given moment if I stay tuned. I adore every one: "More Than a Feeling," "Daydream Believer," "Baby, I Love Your Way," "Ain't No Sunshine."

Yes! Yes! Play any one of those in its entirety! I would be ever so grateful. I hate working out. A good song lets me loathe it less.

I am salivating over the snippets. But after they return from the commercial break they play..."Jack and Diane." Okay. I'm sorry. For me, this is like putting filet mignon on the menu and then serving me a hot dog. This is my opinion and I am entitled to it. I am annoyed. It's a classic bait and switch! They deserve a consequence. I switch to STAR. I would rather listen to the ever-irritating Axl Rose—fingernails on a chalkboard (my opinion again). But, at least they didn't lead me to believe it would be anything else.

I leave the gym and head out for the rest of my day. Jack and Diane follow me around (both of them) everywhere I go—my mani-pedi, Trader Joe's. They assault me from an adjacent car. It's torture. It's like a booger I can't get off my finger.

There's a "sinkhole" on Mulholland Drive (a new word in my Laurel Canyon vocabulary, which means an extra deep and ridiculously wide pothole, usually the result of non-stop rain). Everyone is taking the same detour. Traffic is a mess. But it's okay, because "Light My Fire" (the José Feliciano version—most romantic cover of all time) is on K-EARTH and I absolutely *love* the José Feliciano version of "Light My Fire," especially in the rain. Correction…I *don't* love it, as Alvy Singer put it to Annie Hall, I "lurve" it. That's one step deeper than love. But José is not coming in clearly because I'm in the canyon and just how much you lurve a song can be measured by the amount of static you can withstand and still not change the station. I don't want to abandon "Light My Fire," but just for a millisecond I check KLOS and I hear hints of "Angie." I absolutely adore "Angie" more than anything!

What to do? I am being pulled in opposite directions and I am in an acute state of distress. Shelly's Choice. I will have them both if I can, for as long as they'll have me. José is coming in stronger now, so I stick with him and I pray that when he's through Mick will still be there waiting for me, even if it's just a few last words. *Come on, Mick, they can't say I never tried!* Pleeeeze! When I attempt to reclaim "Angie," it's not only over; it's John Cougar Mellencamp…"Jack and Diane."

Red lights seem longer today. On comes "Bennie and the Jets" and I don't mind the wait. Then, when I get to my daughter's school, something incredible happens while I'm twiddling my thumbs in the carpool lane: "Rich Girl." Thank You Universe. And then "Get Back," and next, The Raspberries, "Go All the Way" (shortest verse ever). I crank it like I'm seventeen and I just got my driver's license. So loud it makes my body buzz. I am Meg Ryan in that famous scene from *When Harry Met Sally* where she's slapping the table, faking a you-know-what, and shouting, "Yes! Yes!" And a diner at another table remarks in envy, "I'll have what she's having."

Then I turn it down, because I remember where I am. Any second, my daughter is going to emerge from those gates and see my car vibrating and hear me shrieking at the top of my lungs (about going all the way, no less). She will be mortified beyond repair and I will be anointed the worst parent in the history of the human race. That's okay, because in the course of a day, whatever the task, pleasant or not, wherever the sinkholes divert me, there's no doubt: *Songs make everything better.*

P.S. I finally got satellite. No static at all.

Don't Bore Us, Get to the Chorus

USUALLY I ARRIVE at a writing session with an idea or a title or a concept in my pocket…something I've wanted to write about for a while. Occasionally, there's nothing in particular on my mind and if no one else has anything on theirs, we are writing from a place called "scratch." This can be terrifying.

I am in awe of writers who tackle the chorus first…writers who excavate for that golden nugget and work backwards from there. There are some rewards to this: the main one being that if you have the heart of the song in place, you can relax, stop worrying and enjoy fishing for verses to support it.

Verses, however, come easily to me. And when they do, I am comforted when I look down and see *something* on my plate…a vegetable or two, if not the entrée. The thought of having an empty plate for an extended period of time, say an hour into a session, makes me feel anxious—like what if I never find my main course? And so, I tend to jump right into those carrots and Brussels sprouts.

A lot of my co-writers love the way I channel verses. I can be very in the moment, but it's risky. Verses *can* easily lead to a chorus, but if and when they don't, I can paint us into a corner and we may never get out.

What a Girl Wants (The Movie)

GUY ROCHE AND I were feeling very puffed up. *What a Girl Wants* was the working title of a Warner Bros. film in production. Now you can't copyright a title, and, because of that, the studio could have called the film *What a Girl Wants* and not paid us a dime as long as the song did not appear in the film. That was not their intention, however. They *wanted* to use the song in the film. And that wasn't all, they wanted an "exclusive," which meant (should we agree to an exclusive) we couldn't grant a license to any other project until *this* film was released. For *that* there was an extra *big fat fee*. Hence, our chests felt full; so did our pockets.

This was new territory for me. I had never before been offered such a substantial sum for the use of a song in a film. I can't deny I fantasized about some indulgences, as well as the dent that could be made in Layla's college education fund.

"Andrea," the Music Supervisor, (someone who oversees the placement of songs in film and television) was an acquaintance of mine. Not a BFF, but a trusted ally. She was excited to bring this placement to the table...to deliver the good news...to be the messenger for such a *mitzvah*.

Guy and I anticipated the congratulatory phone calls from friends who would see the name of our song on movie posters plastered all over Sunset Boulevard. We went on an outing to the Warner lot and had a tourist take a photo of us beneath one of those huge billboards. We looked forward to

That's tiny Guy and me beneath the huge billboard.
Sadly, the film studio would not give me permission to use the poster.

our fifteen minutes of fame on the red carpet. In the months between the request and the release of the film, I stayed in touch with Andrea, if just to hear her reiterate how grand this all was.

On the night of the industry screening, Guy and I meandered through the VIP crowd of entertainment business heavies and studio heads. We made sure they heard (or at least overheard) us shamelessly promoting ourselves as the writers of the song that inspired the film, even though that wasn't exactly true. We tried our best to sound casual and off the cuff. We got our free popcorn and soon everybody took their seats.

The curtain went up. The opening credits rolled. The movie commenced; a song or two went by. No "What a Girl Wants" yet.

That's okay. There's plenty of time. We are the reason for it all!

More songs. "Heaven Is a Place on Earth," "Happy Birthday." The plot thickened. "London Calling." No "What a Girl Wants." Hmm. *Here comes the montage.*

Perfect! I love a good montage! "What a Girl" must be the accompaniment to the montage! Bring it on!

Nope. No "What a Girl Wants" in the montage. Huh?

Nearing the end, one more song, "Because You Loved Me." And then the movie was pretty much over. Guy and I looked at each other perplexed. We figured "What a Girl Wants" had to be the end title song—the song that plays in the most coveted spot of all—while the end credits roll. It wasn't. I assured him that there must be a *second* end title song. (How is that for optimism?) Film studios sometimes like to give the ticket buyer bang for their buck and pack in as many songs as possible—saving the best one for the very, very last!

Alas…our song didn't appear there either. We were the reason for nothing. The theatre emptied. We stayed in our seats and watched the curtain come down. Humbled yet again. The house lights came on and we trudged up the inclined aisle, which felt a lot steeper than it actually was, crossed the now-empty lobby strewn with popcorn, and exited into the night air. I guess we had bragged too much and God said, "Ha."

There were so many questions. Why didn't Andrea tell us? How could she forget? Do we go to the afterparty? And then the most horrifying question of all, which came to us as we emerged from the fog of our wounded egos: *What about the money?* That *Big Fat Fee?*

"Ok, let's not panic," I told Guy. "We'll make some calls first thing in the morning." For now, we would go to the afterparty with as much dignity as we could muster. And, we would have many cocktails.

As it turned out, much to our relief, if an agreement stipulates that the studio will pay an exclusive fee in exchange for a song being kept off the market, and the song *is* kept off the market, the studio has to pay the fee whether they use it or not. This didn't un-bruise our egos, but it sure helped everything else. It's the most I ever got paid for nothing.

P.S. Andrea's name was changed because it might appear that she did me a disservice, but that is absolutely not the case.

Turn the Page

VERY OFTEN, A pre-existing hit is licensed for use in a film in order to propel the story or enhance a scene. I'm grateful for that. (See previous vignette.) One of my favorite songs in a movie? The somber, orchestrated version of Joni Mitchell's "Both Sides Now" in *Love Actually.* In the scene, Emma Thompson escapes to the privacy of her bedroom to compose herself after she opens a Christmas gift that she assumed was a necklace from her husband, which she happened to witness him purchase. It turns out it's a Joni Mitchell CD. She realizes he gave that necklace to someone else.

I would have cried along with teary Emma if there were absolutely no music at all. But *with* "Both Sides Now," a song that makes me cry all by itself, I am inconsolable.

Sometimes, however, directors choose to go with something written specifically *for* the film. In that case, a music supervisor might ask an independent writer, such as myself, to pen something. Back in the day, they'd even pay us to *try.*

In 1999, music supervisor Sharon Boyle was working on the film *Music of the Heart* and asked me to take a shot at writing a song for the opening scene. Full disclosure: Sharon lived across the street from me and we had two-year-old daughters who were playmates. So even though we sipped chardonnay on Friday night while the girls watched *Aladdin,* and hiked on the weekends, I'm quite certain that when she asked me to write something, it wasn't just because we were pals; she believed I was up to the task. It was nice to know it wasn't a cattle call. Psychologically, that makes a difference to a writer. It instills confidence. I could relax. Carefully consider. Take my time.

On a quiet evening when Adam was out and Layla was sleeping, I slipped the tape into my VCR and pressed "play." There on the screen was a heavy-hearted Meryl Streep flipping through a photo album filled with pictures of her and the husband who had recently left her. For me, Meryl is to acting what Carly is to songwriting. She had me imagining what it would feel like if the someone *I* thought would always be there, suddenly wasn't. If the partner I depended on, changed his mind. If Adam pulled up his anchor, how painful to revisit all those memories of "us" in a photo album. I heard a cadence in my head and scribbled down some lines:

> *When I look back,*
> *You're everywhere.*
> *Turn the page,*
> *You were there.*

Nothing clever or fancy. I wrote what I saw, what I felt.

The next day I convened with my trusted collaborator Guy. Guy had a look at my passage and we slid into gear—two passengers on the same ride. Sharon shared "Turn the Page" with the studio, which, in turn, asked up-and-coming recording artist Aaliyah to sing it. Aaliyah's voice was sultry and emotional. You believed her. It's very unusual for everything to fall into place so organically.

The sad part though is how, in this case, life imitated art. The promising young Aaliyah lost her life a year later in a plane crash. Now, when I listen to her sing "Turn the Page," I can't help but feel some kind of eerie prophecy…

> *What would I do if some strange morning*
> *I opened up my eyes to find you gone…*

Snapshot: Fast Car

It's 1988 in New York, I am stepping out of the shower and wrapping myself in a towel. I hear someone singing a song called "Fast Car" from the TV in the next room. I'm thinking, who *is* that guy? I was about to get ready for bed, but that's not going to happen. I can*not* go on living until I hear that hypnotic guitar riff again. I throw on my sweat pants and leather jacket and walk the ten blocks south on Broadway to Tower Records to buy the cassette. I see a face on the packaging. *What?* Tracy Chapman is a *woman?* Okay by me. Even better. I rip off the shrink-wrap and lay the rectangular piece of plastic into my Walkman. I listen to "Fast Car" non-stop on the way back to my apartment. Can't get enough. Now I can sleep.

Where Have All the Albums Gone?

THE WALLS IN my office are filled with Gold and Platinum records. These plaques are awarded by the RIAA (Recording Industry Association of America) to those who contributed in some way to albums that had sales of over 500,000 and 1 million units respectively. I have a lot of them. I'm not saying this boastfully; I've been busy for the last thirty years. Until recently, writers would come by to work with me and not make a big deal about them because it wasn't unusual to see Gold and Platinum records. They might even have had some of their own. However, lately there's a younger crop of writers coming onto the scene (and into my house), who are in awe of my plaques. Why? Because albums aren't selling like they used to.

In 2003 the iTunes store opened its virtual doors. Customers could download any track digitally for ninety-nine cents. For songwriters this was better than the "free" that Napster had been charging, but it led to yet another development.

When iTunes began to flourish, the full-length album started to lose its relevance. We began listening to music *a la carte*—opting out of a more comprehensive experience. Don't get me wrong, as a songwriter I am in constant pursuit of creating a commercially viable, irresistibly infectious, three-minute single. Within the initial context of iTunes, I lived for the possibility of 2 million (paid for) downloads. But, as a listener and a baby boomer, it's bittersweet to watch the album concept and format expire.

Looking back, the "long-playing" album was a ride the artist took me on…*Goodbye Yellow Brick Road, Dog & Butterfly, Silk Degrees, Songs in the Key of Life.* *Every* song was nutritious, even the ones (especially the ones) sandwiched in-between some of the delectable no-brainer singles. They were arranged in a certain order for a reason. They had an emotional arc: I started somewhere, traveled someplace. There was a departure *and* a return. When one side was over, the needle would slide back and forth over the wide slippery groove. I'd lift it up and flip the disc over. And when side two was finished, I'd clip the arm back into its holder, marking the end of my journey. How many hot summer nights did I spend laying on my twin bed transported to another world? There were no spoiler alerts. Nothing got leaked on the Internet. It was all *brand new.* Dinner could wait.

I cherished the cover art and the liner notes—chock full of credits, names of songwriters, musicians, and producers right there at my finger-tips. Details I didn't even know existed. And then there was the intimacy of touching, holding, studying (and, yes, hugging) a tangible album cover. I will forever associate *Anticipation* with a shaggy-haired Carly in that sheer skirt holding on to the gates on either side of her, and *Tapestry*, with curly-haired Carole sitting on that window seat with the cat. Every now and then, I open the cabinet where my vinyl collection rests in peace. It's reassuring, for some reason, to see it's still there. I slide one or two out and run my palm over the dusty jacket—the corners of *Abandoned Luncheonette*…soft and worn from handling—a wine stain here—a cigarette burn there. You can't get that with plastic or digital. Cardboard absorbs memories.

Years later, the CD certainly wasn't as tactile but the full story was there for the taking if I wanted to hear it. And I usually did.

And what of the record *store?* It wasn't so much a warehouse that stocked merchandise, as it was a wonderland of discovery. If I saw a cute guy I might peer over his shoulder to check out what he was interested in. I might get chatty. Maybe we'd go out for coffee sometime and talk about that record. Once I overheard a Swedish shopper ask a salesperson where he could find "Howtie and the Bluefish." Fond memories indeed.

But conceivably this *isn't* as much about the physical discs, or the retail, or the ride, as it is about my own personal pining for the way…I'm just going to say it…it used to be—the way music used to function in my life. A friend of mine suggests that what I am pining for is simply my youth itself. I pause. I ponder this. Indeed, music ushered me through those confusing times and helped me make it out alive and enriched. And, although I still turn to music to move me, maybe I no longer depend on it to heal me, to find me, steer me, define me. Perhaps there is some truth to what my friend says. Wow. Okay.

If that's the case, I still can't help but want for my daughter the same escape that I once cherished: an urgent desire to hang a "do not disturb" sign on my bedroom door knowing I would soon be sucked into that delicious vortex through which only an album could take me.

Today's teens may not miss what they never had. I can't argue with that. So maybe I should just feel grateful that I was lucky enough to have had it.

If walls could talk…in my office with Chris Sernel.

So Sue Me X3

ON A SNOWY winter day, back in 1994, I willed my little engine that could up a five-hundred-foot snow covered driveway and arrived at the palatial home of David Bryan, keyboard player in Bon Jovi. He had been a dedicated member of the extremely successful band for many years and it had obviously paid off.

We wrote a song that day called "Damned." The idea was "I'm *damned* if I do, *damned* if I don't (love you)." It definitely had potential. With the right artist, it could fly. David said he would play it for Jon. Maybe Jon would want to cut it. Excellent. *That* could give it wings.

Jon passed. I was bummed, but by this time I was immune to rejection. I had made a friend in David and life went on. But when Bon Jovi's album came out, I couldn't help but notice a song on it called…Can you guess? Exactly.

I listened to Bon Jovi's "Damned." Musically it was quite different from the "Damned" David and I had written, but the concept *was*…"Damned if you love me, damned if you don't." I'd say *that* was similar.

At the very least I needed to vent, so I called David and said something like, "Dude…what is *up* with that?" And he said something like, "Yeah, I know!" And I said something like, "Well, did you play him our song or not?" And he said something like, "Yeah." I said, "So aren't you gonna *say*

something?" And he said something like, "I can't, man. He's my paycheck."
Ahh.

Now, you can't copyright a title or an expression or an idea. And of course the *same* idea *could* have been bouncing around in *Jon's* head too. No law against that. But if it *was* bouncing around in his head, it was a *colossal* coincidence.

So I thought, geez! Okay…well, I'm gonna call my publisher and vent to them. It's part of their job to receive my vent. Little Hit & Run Music had not been sold yet, but at this point it was conducting business under the roof of a major. So unfortunately, it wasn't Suzan that I would be venting to. When I called it was business as usual. I was told, quite matter-of-factly, something to the effect of, "Shelly, we publish Jon too. We can't touch this." Of course they couldn't. Who would they rather piss off? Let me think. Shelly? Or Jon Bon Jovi?

I'm well aware that all songwriters (myself included) hear a song sometimes and think…*"One day I'd like to write my own version of that."* Our antennae are always up. We can't account to everyone who has inspired us or influenced our creativity; we'd be broke. We *can*, however, voluntarily share the credit with someone by whom we might have *been* influenced, especially if it's someone who's been playing in our band for so many years. It all very well might have been a colossal coincidence. I can't prove anything, but you know what I think.

Forever Young

LAYLA WAS TODDLING about the house, sippy cup in tow, waving a fairy wand squealing, "What Girl Wants, What Girl Needs." I couldn't shut her off. She had entered that girly girl princess phase where her world revolved around pink plastic kitten heels and Ariel mermaid costumes. Every song I wrote was her mantra. It was delightful to be adored. And this delight poetically replaced my previous trepidations about embarking on parenthood. When she got a little older, a number of tween divas like Ashley Tisdale and Miranda Cosgrove came to work with me, and Layla would ask to have a picture taken with them (the apple doesn't fall far). Then she'd patter away.

One day she came home from school to find "Hannah Montana" in the living room. She sat down on the floor with her back up against the wall, arms hugging her knees with absolutely no intention of pattering *anywhere*.

"Layla, don't you have homework, honey?"

She shook her head, mouth open, eyes glazed over and transfixed on Miley Cyrus. She wasn't moving. Maybe I should have told Layla before she went to school that day that her favorite TV star would be there when she came home. As if that would have given a nine-year-old girl the maturity to compose herself. It was all good; Miley was used to this.

Ironically, Layla was a welcome diversion from the obvious generation gap between Miley and myself. (My relationships to artists were starting to resemble the storyline of *The Curious Case of Benjamin Button. They* were getting younger and younger, while *I* was getting older. I couldn't have been the only one who noticed.)

Layla with "Hannah."

In middle school, Layla went through a songwriting stage herself. Honesty is effortless in seventh grade. The songs may not be structured or tight, but man can they tell the truth—nothing in the way yet...no over-thinking. My daughter came up with some enviable song titles. So, when I felt like my well was running a little dry, because I had other things on my mind like vaccines and sunscreen and blessings of skinned knees, I considered borrowing titles like "Butterfly," and imagining it was an idea *I* had come up with myself. (Not unlike Jon Bon You-Know-Who.)

Eventually, Layla's excitement at the thought of coming home to find young pop stars in her house started wearing off as her tastes were moving on to the likes of The Fray and The Script. There was a bit of a rebound though, with "American Idol" runner-up, David Archuleta. It wasn't because she was star-struck though; it was because they were mutual fans of bands I'd never even heard of. After working with David one afternoon, I was about to drop him off at his friend's house and Layla wanted to come along for the ride. The two of them climbed into the backseat and didn't shut up. I was their chauffeur—not even there.

Layla and her buddy, David Archuleta.

Not too long ago, I played Layla a song and asked her for her opinion. She shrugged and mustered an "It's okay." Do you know what's worse than someone at a record label telling you your song sucks? Your fifteen-year-old telling you your song sucks. Soon after that, I stopped asking her what she thought. Why open myself up to the rejection? She's over me. Wake up Dorothy, this isn't Radio Disney any more.

Jesse McCartney might have been the equivalent to my mother bringing home Bobby Sherman, or, may he rest in peace, Davy Jones.

Snapshot: What's Love Got to Do with It?

I had a chance to work with Terry Britten, writer of Tina Turner's smash, "What's Love Got to Do with It." I was in awe, not because it was such a big hit, but because it was such a great song. Well, okay, because it was a big hit too. After all those years of pondering the sarcasm, I finally got the opportunity to ask Terry if he really believed that love was overrated…a hindrance rather than a blessing. "What *does* love have to do with it, Terry?" I asked. To which he humbly replied, "Everything."

Nashville

WHEN PEOPLE ASK me if I go to Nashville, I say, "Sorry, I'm allergic." That's a bit of an exaggeration. It's also what I say about wearing the color green. It's not that I don't like Nashville or the color green; they just don't look good on me. I'm a fish out of water in Nashville, and though I know it's healthy to venture out of your comfort zone once in a while, there are some places you might find you are just *too* uncomfortable.

Traditional country music has always been about "the song." You have to respect that. Although there's a lot more than just country music being written in Nashville lately, even the new breed of country sticks to relatively straightforward chord progressions. I prefer them a bit more left of center, unpredictable. And I like the abstract and ethereal rather than the strong story line. Certainly, this has a lot to do with what I grew up listening to. There's no right or wrong. It's a matter of taste. Beauty is in the ears of the beholder.

On my first writing trip to Nashville (and to be fair this was some time ago), I was advised not to use certain words...like "baby" unless it was actually an infant to which I was referring. And I was told to use as much "furniture" as possible.

"Furniture?"

"Oh you know, the steam rising from your coffee cup, the strings on your guitar. Your truck. Your beer."

"Oh, *visuals*. And that's a rule? And you call it furniture?"

"Yeah, the more the merrier."

Furniture for the sake of furniture? A dining room table—a La-Z-Boy? I am more of a confessional girl. I talk about the messy things going on in my heart. If what's going on has nothing to do with steam rising from my coffee, I can't make anyone believe it does. You'd know I was faking. Trust me.

Those boundaries and rules have relaxed since then, but that was my first experience writing a country song and I obviously haven't gotten over it.

On one of our ventures to Nashville, Suzan and I had a memorable meeting with Susan Nadler at Asylum Records. We literally had a squabble in her office *while* we were pitching her what we thought could pass for country. Suzan asserted the song *I* played was dated and had too much reverb. *I was so over* the song *she* played (even though I wrote it). It was so *not* country. We were trying to out country each other and the truth is neither one of us had an ounce of country in us. Susan Nadler didn't know what hit her. Neither did her little dog that was running around the office yapping and growling. He must have smelled the impostors.

I have never once in my entire career had a song recorded in Nashville as a result of going there with the intention of writing one for a country artist. Maybe that's karma, because I was trying to write for a genre to which I didn't even relate. Trying to make someone I didn't even love...love me back—not cool. Every country cut I ever got came from out of the blue and was a gift. Reba, Keith, Mark, Deanna…I thank you from the bottom of my love seat, I mean futon…I mean, heart. I really do. I am honored.

I haven't been to Nashville in years. I have to believe that natives can tell when you're trying to fake their accent. So, out of respect, I don't try to fit my square peg in their round hole anymore. It's disingenuous. I can't write a country song. I'll leave it to those who can. I do, however, love and miss the hospitality, the running track on the Vanderbilt campus and the deep-fried oysters at South Street.

P.S. There are country writers who come to L.A. hoping to write pop songs. They think their ideas will fit right in and we'll be able to get them a cut with Kelly or Katy. Let's be honest, pop writers: we have our own sneaky agendas in these sessions. We try to skew the song country so maybe they'll take it back home and get us a big fat cut with Blake or Carrie. All the piggybacking has become pretty obvious. Currently, there is an unspoken "whoever bought the ticket" rule: If a country writer pays for a trip to L.A., we respectfully write a pop song. And if we pay for the ticket to Nashville, it's country all the way, or as country as we can fake it.

Stumbling

NATASHA BEDINGFIELD WAS standing at the mic having trouble singing my song, "Stumble," because she didn't feel that the first line, *"I'm not the kind of girl you'd bring to mother,"* was something she'd say. I guess her logic was that she absolutely *was* the kind of girl you'd bring to mother (sweet, smart, wholesome).

I didn't blame Natasha. The song was about an odd girl who exposed someone for having a crush on her. It probably *wasn't* part of her story. However, the label's Keith Naftaly (to whom Suzan pitched the song) felt strongly about "Stumble" and I wasn't about to talk him out of it. I tried this reasoning with her: *"What if you didn't think of the girl in the song as peculiar? But rather, someone who was about to become a Superstar?* (Which Natasha was.) *Not every mother would want her son bringing home a celebrity, right? So 'not the girl you bring to mother' makes sense."* Kinda. She wasn't buying it.

Respectfully, my co-writer, producer Greg Wells and I tried to come up with an alternative. We wanted Natasha to be happy. The last word of a new line had to at least rhyme softly with the last word of the second line, which was *"I'm not the kind of girl you'd kiss in public."* Also…it had to be good. Nothing worked. To be frank, I *loved* that opening line. It's the thought that had set the whole song in motion—one of those lines that just popped into my head, after which much of the rest of the song effortlessly unfolded.

It was getting late and many hours had passed. She still hadn't sung the line. Greg and I weren't sure what to do. But then Keith stopped by to hear the progress, and miraculously, the air in the studio changed. He must have had some strong positive chi, because she got on the mic and sang the line as written.

Two albums later, Natasha released a single called "Strip Me." I can't help but wonder what *mother* thought about that.

Greg Wells and Natasha.

Snapshot: Creep

It's 1992. Radiohead is all the rage. Haven't we all felt like that "Creep" at some point in our lives? The outcast? Please say "yes." *This* creep is the most lovely, poetic heady creep ever. If I was at that party he wasn't invited to and he told me my *skin makes him cry* and I *float like a feather in a beautiful world*—game over. I'd take him home.

Tom & Delilah

MOZELLA, A QUIRKY soulful pop artist, who wore her blond hair in cone-shaped buns on either side of her head (Princess Leia style) was making an album on Maverick Records. She and I convened with Jude Cole—a gifted recording artist himself—to write something for it. As it was Mozella's voice for which we were writing, Jude and I gave her right-of-way. She came with an idea that started out like a letter: *"Dear Michael… please believe me, sometimes I can't let go."* She was giving cred to her boo for teaching her how to love. Her real live boo's name (at the time) *was* Michael.

"Gavin," Mozella's creative point person at Maverick, insisted we lose the "Michael." He thought a personal name was too specific and the general listening public would not relate. Umm…Billy Jean, Alison, Peggy Sue? *What are you saying? Only people who have those names are capable of appreciating those songs?* Daniel, Jude, Cecilia? He was adamant. He said he wouldn't include our song, "Love is Something," on the record if we left it as is. We acquiesced. We *"genericized"* our song and removed the Michael, but personally I felt it was a lot less interesting, and so did Mozella and Jude. And we were right.

A funny thing happened shortly after that unpleasant concession. There was a huge hit on the radio called, "Hey There Delilah." It was written by my friend, Tom Higgenson, of Plain White T's.

Mozella.

TOM AND I had met a few years earlier. He had reluctantly come to my house, unsure he wanted to have *SongSex*. My philosophy has always been, "let's just jam and if we don't trip on something we love, we'll order a pizza and we'll have made a friend." It's not passive-aggressive, I swear. Knowing it's okay if we come up empty-handed puts everyone at ease (including me). But, Tom and I *did* like what we tripped on that day. We called it, "All That We Needed," *and* we had pizza and made a friend. "All That We Needed" became the title track on Plain White T's debut album on Fearless Records. The last song on that record was "Hey There Delilah." You wouldn't have known that, however, unless you bought the whole album and listened to every song, because "Delilah" had never been on the radio. Yet.

When the band was making their *next* album on their new label, Hollywood Records', Bob Cavallo (head of the label) felt Plain White T's had missed an opportunity by not releasing the delightful "Delilah" as a single. He wanted to include it on the *new* album so that Hollywood Records *could*. Nice to know someone had the balls to re-issue the same song by the same band two albums in a row.

One night I was pulling into my driveway and something very familiar came on the radio. I knew that song (and that voice), because unlike many, I *had* listened to every track on that first album. It was "Hey There Delilah"— on KROQ, no less, a modern rock station where you'd rarely hear a song that didn't feature drums and loud guitars. "Delilah" was delicate—just an acoustic guitar and Tom's honest voice. It became a *big fat hit* and reached No.1 on the *Billboard* Hot 100. Apparently, a lot of people who weren't named Delilah loved it.

About a year later, I attended a dinner where Plain White T's performed for a crowd honoring Bob Cavallo. I was proud of Tom. (I don't know why; I had nothing to do with the success of his song.) Maybe I was just happy that it defied the odds. After the band played, I made my way backstage and found him. I wanted to say, "Look at you with that *big fat hit!*" Surprisingly, Tom wouldn't stop going on about "Bitch." I said, "Dude, shut *up*. Radio wants tempo, booty calls, female empowerment anthems! You wrote this simple romantic ode to your boo (and gave the boo a name) and they're playing it on KROQ! And everywhere else! Seriously, give yourself some credit!"

Artists have moments of brilliance, and days when they can't find their zone. Sometimes they're brilliant *and* in their zone at the same time, and they have no clue. (In my opinion, Tom was in that place when he wrote "Delilah.") An artist is lucky to be surrounded by trusted allies at labels who let him know (tactfully) when he could do better, and who recognize her brilliance when she loses perspective. I bet if Mozella had been on Hollywood Records, Bob would have said, "Leave the Michael in." I wish someone had been there to overrule Gavin.

Songwriter/producer Ian Kirkpatrick and Plain White T's: Michael Retondo, Dave Tirio, Tom Higgenson, (Me), Tim Lopez, De'Mar Hamilton.

P.S. This vignette is dedicated to: Alison, Elenore, Barbara Ann, Mandy, Layla, Lola, Michelle, Roxanne, Angie, Brandy, Johnny B, Abraham, Martin, John, Walk Away Renee, Jessie's Girl, Bobby's Girl, Rosalinda, Sharona, Jimmy Mack, Levon, Louie, Sherry Baby, Baby James, Mrs. Jones, Mrs. Robinson, Miss Molly, Bobby McGee, Ben, Julia, Prudence, Lucy, Bungalow Bill, Sexy Sadie, Martha, Maxwell, Lovely Rita…and yes, Jack and Diane.

P.P.S. Mozella went on to write "Wrecking Ball" for Miley Cyrus. I guess she knew what she was doing. Rumor has it Gavin is selling real estate in Texas.

Ch-Ch-Ch-Ch-Changes

FOR THE MOST part over the years, when I've written a song with someone, whether it was a recording artist or a fellow serial songwriter, they were in the room with me…sleeves rolled up, rubbing their hands together—ready to go. Something happened while I was busy enjoying writing songs with other human beings. And it took me a minute to notice: the craft of songwriting took a sharp left turn and I woke up in a neighborhood I hardly recognized. Fasten your seat belts. I will explain.

Once upon a time, a "record producer" was a captain of sorts whose expertise entailed visualizing how a song should sound and bringing it to life while keeping the artist engaged and inspired throughout the process. The song was the star of the show. The producer delegated tasks, hired talented players, arrangers and engineers, all in the service of doing justice to the *song*, capturing the magic, and making a hit record. This was a special gift. Labels valued producers and they were compensated generously for this job alone. Some of the names are legendary—George Martin, Phil Ramone, Quincy Jones. Their talent was separate from songwriting. Producers weren't expected to be songwriters, although some, quite naturally and understandably, were.

All this was before it was possible for songs to be constructed without any live musicianship. Back when nothing happened inside a computer. If you wanted drums you had to hire a drummer. The idea that there would ever be a musical track *before* a song didn't exist. Now it does.

With the advance of digital technology, an audio programmer could now create a musical bed of beats and sounds called a "backing track" and offer it up as a *template* for a song. A programmer could then fuse his backing track with an irresistibly hooky "topline" (the melody and lyric—more about this shortly) and potentially get hired to make the record. They'd get paid a fee to be in the driver's seat (albeit much less than a conventional captain would have been) *and,* since they created the backing track that inspired the song at hand, they would own a piece of the writing as well.

With programmers at the helm, the traditional producers (the artist whisperers, accomplished visionaries, delegators, therapists and creative muses) started to disappear. The programmers got the job done, but the relationship between them and the artist was often less holistic, more provisional.

It's also worth noting that the birth of the backing track transformed the nature of the song demo. Because electronic programming has become so economical and prevalent, a full-on presentation is expected…bells and whistles…nothing left to the imagination. If I want to dazzle the label with my song, I have to present a dazzling production. So I have a decision to make: I can approach a programmer-*du-jour* and try to hire him (or her— but usually a him) to record a demo, but in the twenty-first century music business it's likely he'll ask for as much as half the songwriting credit instead of a demo fee (even though all the melody and lyric and perhaps even all the chord changes are already in place). Alternately, I *could* reach out to a lesser-known programmer, who is in need of the cash and won't ask for half the copyright, but reality is no matter how dazzling *that* demo turns out, the song probably won't get as much attention simply because lesser-known's name isn't impressive enough.

On rare occasions, I will write something by myself on a piano and play an A&R exec a voice memo and they'll say they get it and, not to worry, and they'll actually hire an independent producer to produce it. I am comforted that they still exist—the independent producer *and* this fading breed of A&R. But I fear it won't be for much longer.

P.S. While backing tracks can be formulaic and mass-produced (which is why so many electronically-based songs on the radio started sounding alike), there are programmers who are more than mere track hacks, ones who are able to participate in other aspects of songwriting—the lyric, the phrasing, the melody, the emotional arc. They absolutely deserve an equal share of the song pie, in addition to their production fee, when a song gets commercially released. Sometimes they even play a real instrument, come up with a title, sing! I love those guys! And they know who they are.

Toplining

THE ARRIVAL OF the backing track not only changed the organic nature of writing a song, it dramatically affected the way a songwriter's contribution is valued. It's not unusual for a backing track to be chosen for a project before there's even a topline attached.

In case you haven't heard: a topline is a millennial term for the *melody and lyric* writers conjure up to go with a backing track given to them (or sent to them electronically) by a programmer, because he needs a plot, clever words, sound bites, and a catchy hook so that his track will have the necessary ingredients to qualify as a song.

As backing track-driven material (especially EDM—electronic dance music) moved to the forefront of pop radio, a writer who wanted to land songs with successful chart-topping artists had no choice but to jump on the bandwagon. A backing track is often just a beat and some sounds that repeat themselves for three minutes with no song form at all. It's up to the topliner to establish the divisions with, for example, changes in phrasing, melodic contour. While a backing track *can* be a more realized structure that inspires a topliner to great heights, either way, all by itself, a backing track is not a song. I can sing you my melody and lyric. Can you sing me your backing track?

So creatively, I have a problem being called a topliner. Not just because it *sounds* trivial, but because it also diminishes *me*. Are the melody and lyrics mere embellishments? Something with which to decorate something *else*? Is that what it has come to?

There is also an economic agenda behind the concept of the "topline" being assimilated into the songwriting zeitgeist. In the past, songwriting credit and royalties were divided between the melody and the lyric. Everything else on a recording was the "arrangement." (You wrote the song first and then the producer got the guys and gals in to play it.) In essence, the topline *was the song*.

As the economics of the music business became more desperate, all parties were scrambling for every dollar. If the status of the melody and lyric could be relegated to a supporting role relative to the importance of a sonically tasty backing track, the programmer (and therefore his/her manager, publisher, and accountant) could now claim a share of the songwriting pie.

And there it is. The food chain reconfigured:

1. The Programmer was upgraded to *Producer*

2. The Programmer became a *Songwriter* as well

3. The Artist formerly known as a Songwriter was now merely a *Topliner*

This is quite an adjustment for many of us who've dedicated our lives to a more organic process of crafting a song. But, I am a journeyman, and it's clear that toplining is firmly planted in the modern-day songwriting process. I can and I will topline; I'm no fool. Hit records are more production-oriented than ever. When the time comes that they aren't, I'll recalibrate for that too. But I'd be hard-pressed to deny my delight at opening the front door to find some dude or chick standing there with a smile and a guitar. Although I am rolling with the changes as best I can, I believe if you can sing something *a capella*—*that* is a *song*, perhaps not a hit record, but a song. Whereas, a backing track is simply waiting to become one.

17 Minutes of Britney

BRITNEY SPEARS USED to live about a mile away from my house in a gated community called The Summit. (She doesn't live there anymore, so please don't go trying to find her.) There wasn't a day that you'd drive over Mulholland when there wasn't an assemblage of black SUVs parked on the shoulder, a photographer leaning against each one, Starbucks cup in hand, waiting for a glimpse…ready to ambush Britney with shutter clicks and "Over heres!" A full body shot would be optimum, but a toe or an earlobe would suffice. (Someone got really lucky with that well-publicized crotch shot.)

I was excited that Britney was going to record my song "Out from Under" for her forthcoming album, *Circus.* This was one of those little miracles I never take for granted. I had been given a full piece of music, melody included, for which I was asked to write a lyric with Britney in mind. Admittedly, when I wrote the words I was projecting how it might have felt to be trying to get over someone. Perhaps someone named Justin. It was a little presumptuous of me, I know, but projection and presumption are good song starters.

On the night she was going to cut vocals, I was on my way to the studio (not only was I invited, I was expected) and I passed all the SUVs and hungry paparazzi. It just so happened *I* knew where Britney was, and where she *was,* was where *I* was going. For once, I felt like I knew something they didn't. I watched them get smaller and smaller in my rear-view mirror as I drove further and further away.

I wasn't as exclusively in the loop as I thought though, because when I arrived at Glenwood Studios, the street was mobbed with yet *another* horde of paparazzi that knew *exactly* where Britney was. I made my way through the door only to find a celebrity news show on a flat screen in the lounge with footage of those same paparazzi outside in the street. She can't escape.

Inside the control room, Britney was sweet if not particularly sociable. She was a trooper at the mic doing multiple takes when necessary…a singer with her own unique vibe…as opposed to a belter with perfect pitch, multiple octave range, and enviable melisma. She was spaced-out and detached yet mysteriously emotional, and delicate, and vulnerable. So *what* if the engineer tuned and comped the vocals (made a composite of the best lines by cherry-picking and piecing together the best phrases, even syllables, in order to achieve that ultimate "one take" performance). The girl has a gift. There's a reason she's a star.

There was talk that "Out from Under" might be released as an international single. Eventually, when push came to shove, I was told that Britney was not in favor of it—the song made her seem *too* vulnerable. *What's wrong with vulnerable? You do vulnerable so well!* Maybe she thought her fans would think "Out from Under" *was* about Justin and perhaps she had moved on. Or maybe it was too close to the truth. In any case, that's what I get for projecting and presuming. I had had high hopes for "Out from Under," but it was what it was, and on *I* moved, ecstatic that it would be included on the album at all.

Upon the release of *Circus,* I was invited to a party in N.Y. to celebrate. I had responsibilities—a carpool schedule, a teachers' conference, yet another song to write. I thought I'd wait until the label threw a party on the left coast, but Suzan told me I was crazy…that I should go bask in the little miracle if only to thank Barry Weiss (the head of the label) for giving my song the nod. As usual she was right. I RSVP'd. I would pay the inflated last-minute airfare, go to N.Y. for two nights, come right back and resume carpool.

The flight was uneventful…the kind you hope for. The cab that took me into the city smelled worse than the tunnel we drove through. But as soon as I stepped out into the N.Y. night, I wondered why I ever left. Funny, I miss New York the most when I'm there. I strolled Columbus Avenue, had dinner with my sister at Carmine's, bought some cheese at Zabar's, slept at my in-laws, jogged around the Central Park reservoir in the morning, strolled Amsterdam Avenue, met my friend Jamie for cocktails, had sushi with my attorney Mark Levinsohn and then, at around 10:00pm, Mark drove me to the extravaganza in the heart of the fashionable meat-packing district.

I had been told there would be no plus ones…that the guest list was "tight." They always say that.

That's okay. Even better. Small party. Maybe I'll get a selfie with Brit. Back in the studio it might have rubbed her the wrong way had I held up my iPhone. But tonight, maybe she'll tell me how much she loves my song…that it's her favorite one on the album, that she's changed her mind and wants it to be a single!

Au contraire. Outside the club, I had to compete with the supermodels to get to the front of the line. My name was on the list but no one seemed to notice. When I was finally granted entrance it was *packed, hot, loud, young*.

I needed to find Teresa, my A&R heroine who had fallen in love with my song and was responsible for getting it to Britney. She was on the other side of the Velvet Rope that separated me from The Very Important People. I was stuck in the middle of the Unimportant. Larry Rudolph, Britney's manager, slipped me a wristband, and instantaneously, my status was transformed and I was allowed to cross the Velvet Rope. I was now Very Important and I was closer to Teresa. She threw me a lifeline with her eyes. There was no point in trying to shout above the noise of the crowd.

What am I doing? I could be home in bed watching "Nurse Jackie."

I knew I wasn't long for the party. Who was I kidding? There would be no selfie.

There she was…Britney, the belle of the ball…surrounded by an entourage in a dark corner.

I've never seen nipples so close to the edge of a garment. I swear, I don't know how the girl breathes.

Something was happening. All The Very Important People parted like the Red Sea. It's possible I was hallucinating at this point, but I really don't think so. I'm pretty sure her posse positioned themselves in front and in back of her…hands on each other's shoulders, like a flash mob bunny hop…an impenetrable protective field…a most elaborate escort. Britney had to pee. It was precisely at that moment I decided *Circus* was the perfect name for her new album.

"Where's Barry Weiss?" I shouted to Teresa. She shifted her eyes his way. There he was, on the other side of yet *another* Velvet Rope, chatting away with the Very *Very* Important People. I shot the "rope diplomat" darts with my eyes; he unhooked it and let me pass. I approached Barry. I told him who I was and what I had written. And I thanked him for giving my song the love. He said it was nice to meet me and I believe he meant it. Then, he turned away and started talking to someone else, but my mission was accomplished. I told myself that somewhere in the back of his mind, I had been duly noted. He knew I existed and I wasn't invisible, and then I left. I was at that party for a total of 17 minutes.

I wasn't happy about turning the lights out on N.Y. so quickly. So to extend my forty-eight hour pass, I ventured up 10th Avenue (which wouldn't have been a good idea when I still lived there) and made my way to 43rd Street where George—the boyfriend from college who hid in my closet during that *Baltimore Sun* interview—managed a sports bar. I hadn't seen him in over twenty years and I thought this would be a good time to pop by. He was surprised to say the least. We reminisced about events I never would have remembered had he not reminded me…like a car accident we were in together that had completely evaporated from my brain! (Pass the ginkgo biloba.) I felt badly that he worked at that bar and he lived in a hole in the wall with his dog, in the part of Hell's Kitchen that was still

Hell. But, he was *so* happy to see me, and it felt *good* to be with somebody to whom I mattered.

In the morning, I got myself a Starbucks and went for a walk. I bought a gorgeous red dress that I totally didn't need because I swore I heard it call my name from a store window. That bit of retail therapy took my mind off of the selfie I didn't get with Britney. And then I went to the airport in a *hired car*, because I couldn't take another smelly cab. Uneventful flight home.

For the first couple of years after I left N.Y.C., I'd get disoriented when flying from coast to coast. Upon descent to either side, I couldn't get clear as to whether I was coming or going. This time when I landed in L.A., I knew exactly where I was: I was home. Soon I was back in my bed like I never left: "Nurse Jackie" on TiVo. Tomorrow, on to another song. I hear Britney's making a new album.

Come Together

WHEN I COLLABORATE, because I am a musician, melodist *and* lyricist, I tend to do what my co-writer doesn't. If he plays a badass guitar, or she programs killer tracks, I'll stick to the words. But if he or she doesn't play at all, I'll get behind the keyboard.

Sometimes we are both adept at music *and* lyrics. Personally, I like this arrangement best. It feels most symbiotic.

When I'm writing by myself, the words and the melody *always* reveal themselves simultaneously—the chicken *and* the egg. It's like they belong together. They are in a "relationship." And I don't think that status will ever change.

How Hard Can You Get Me

SINCE THERE ARE fewer and fewer third-party producers (captains) involved in the pop song-making process, and programmers are now being called "producers," regardless of whether they have limited skills or talents abounding, for the sake of simplicity I will hereafter be calling programmers "producers." However, I will put them in "quotation marks" out of respect *for* and to differentiate them *from* the more accomplished variety. Here are some interesting developments of late:

As much as I am troubled by the new normal, I must confess, I developed a taste for writing to "producer"-supplied backing tracks…partly out of necessity…and partly because it *can* be amusing—like casual sex, I don't take it too seriously. I listen on repeat while I'm making dinner or coloring my hair, while I'm on the treadmill, and of course, while I'm driving. I marinate. I simmer. The backing track seeps into my unconscious and, if I'm lucky, by the end of the day, something catchy jumps out at me— an "earworm." And when it does, it's like I've cracked a code. But if it doesn't impress the "producer," he moves on to another topliner—guilt free. Sometimes he doesn't even tell me he's moved on. He doesn't even consider it inconsiderate. It's not his fault. Chances are he's much younger than I am and this practice has been typical since he's entered the game. It's the only way he knows how to play.

Sometimes "producers" solicit hooks for their backing tracks—not full songs—just *prefabricated* hooks. *Or* hooks that songwriters might consider extracting from a pre-existing (already written) song with the hope that the "producer" can deliver it to an artist he is working with, have the artist write her *own* verses and include it on her album as a completely new song.

Then there is the "open call" where a bunch of select topliners are invited to a studio. One-by-one they step up to the mic and have a few minutes to come up with choice bits for the backing track at hand. Sometimes, the "producer" isn't even present. It may just be his assistant running Pro Tools (recording software) on his behalf, collecting all the morsels. The backing track is the *fluffer* and the topliners are the *porn stars. Do we have wood?*

At the end of the session, the "producer" will decide which contributions he'll keep and which ones will end up on the cutting room floor. Maybe he'll use your whole hook, or just one line, or a few words. Then he will allocate percentages of ownership, most likely insisting on taking 50% of the songwriting credit for *himself* because he believes he wrote "all the music," even though there was no melody before *you* walked in the room. The topliners will accept the divisions because, after all, in being there, they are agreeing to the terms. (Can you imagine Burt Bacharach or Cynthia Weil having to play by those rules?)

My more seasoned colleagues and I have an expression for this piecing together of lines and phrases. We call it "Frankenwriting," or writing by committee. I've heard that in many of these sessions itemized lists are distributed that specify the percentage of songwriting credit (royalty) a Frankenwriter will receive for coming up with a particular part. For instance, she might get a full 25% if she writes the hook, 10% if he (guys are topliners too) comes up with the title, 5% for each line in a verse.

Once, I showed up at a studio where I was booked to work one-on-one with a "producer" who supposedly had the "special sauce." He left me in the control room with a backing track on repeat while he went to lunch…alone in a room without any foreplay. I was a sperm donor trying to jerk off into a paper cup, but I was never going to come. By the time he returned, I hadn't even gotten hard. I had absolutely nothing to show for myself, except I was hungry. Special sauce, my ass.

Is it me? I've been trying *to go with the flow. Am I becoming that girl at the party you avoid because I'm such a drag? So negative. Such a whiner. The one who can't shut up about how weird things are. I never wanted to be that girl, Debbie Downer. But I sort of am.*

Suzan saw this coming. For my own good, she suggested that I try to be more dispassionate. The songwriting business (or should I say "song construction business") was changing and if I wanted to stay relevant, I had to make peace with this new terrain. Of course, she was right (again). However, in my fantasy, she told me, *"No!...don't do it. Stay in your lane. Mind your corner."* But she *didn't* say this. Neither did my friends in publishing, many of whom signed and represented the players who rewrote these new rules. If I kept resisting, I just might get left behind—alone in my corner, in my own little chair.

I wondered...if these practices had already been commonplace when *I* came up in the game, would I or would I not see the absurdity? Still, there were some things I just could not do. I could not go to that open call, or allow myself to be assigned credit. Was it beneath me? Was I proud? Yes and yes. But if I *didn't* go, there's one thing I could count on: one more gig I definitely was *not* going to get. I heard people say, "Ten percent of some-thing is more than zero percent of nothing." I swear I wasn't so sure.

Double Dipping

IMAGINE THIS: A "producer" gives you a backing track, but he doesn't tell you you're not the only one he gave it to.

What? That's like not telling me you're dating other people.

He wants to see what kind of topline you'll come up with…and then he'll compare it to everyone else's and decide which he likes best.

What? What about you come over to my house and we have SongSex? Break for lunch…have coffee…talk about life…have some more SongSex?

This is what happened with a favorite "producer" of mine, who shall be called "Lazer." Usually, Lazer and I wrote in the same room together, sleeves-rolled-up style, but on this occasion I happened to fertilize his backing track (which he had emailed to me), and with my words (and melody) we conceived…a song.

I pitched our song for a project and got the approval from the A&R exec. I texted Lazer the excellent news. It was odd that I didn't hear back from him. Songwriters live for that kind of news. Who I finally *did* hear from was Lazer's manager who emailed (not called) to say…"I just want you to be aware that we may need Lazer to change the track a bit, as he may be using it with a different topline for another placement."

What? What happened to a lyric being married to the music? And if you wanted a divorce, you'd at least have a chat. Does the commitment between a topline and a backing track (or a topliner and a "producer" for that matter) fall under a new standard of relaxed betrothal?

I kept texting Lazer...*there must be some mistake...Lazer wouldn't do that to me*...silence.

I'm aware email has no tone, but the manager's correspondence made it sound like it was no big deal. Like it happens every day. But what was I supposed to tell the artist who wanted to record it? What was I supposed to tell the A&R exec? That "after changes are made" to the song they fell in love with it will have a different chord progression? Texture? Character? Beat? And isn't it presumptuous (and offensive) to suggest tracks are substitutable? When I write a melody and lyric (okay...a topline), it's inspired by a particular atmosphere. An alternative atmosphere will not be as logically or emotionally connected to the words.

Let's imagine an alternate scenario: What if I applied the same lyric to two different backing tracks created by two different "producers"? Then, when "producer A" tells me that Selena Gomez wants to record *our* song, I have *Suzan* email him (not call) to say, "Our apologies, but Shelly is actually going to use that lyric on a track she wrote with 'producer B' for Demi Lovato, so we're going to have to change the lyric for Selena. No big deal. Selena won't even notice." "Producer A" would go ballistic, don't you think? And rightly so.

For a while, this behavior was systemic. It wasn't necessarily arrogance, or ignorance, that motivated the disregard for topliners' efforts. It was more like impatience. There was so much competition, and young "producers" got restless waiting for a song to find a home. So, the idea of having multiple partners upped the chances of conceiving a viable song with *one of them* and bringing it to term.

It was naive of me to assume that a pre-existing backing track was monogamous, even if it came from Lazer...my buddy. I should have known better.

I was disappointed about what happened, because I enjoyed writing with Lazer. Don't get me wrong; I hate all the track-flinging. But I was willing to say, "Hey, Laze…from now on can we write from the ground up? We've done it before." Surely, he enjoyed working with me too! He said so *all* the time.

But Lazer remained MIA. I saw him at a Christmas party and he wouldn't look me in the eye. I'm not sure if he felt bad, if he didn't feel responsible at all, or if he just didn't want to deal. After all, it *was* Christmas. Whatever the reason, I'm pretty sure he thought *I* was the freak.

Kum Ba Yah

THERE'S BEEN A trend in the pop song-making business where a record label or a publishing company or even an enterprising producer organizes a "writing camp," an event where a bevy of handpicked topliners and programmers are invited to participate in a songwriting marathon for a few days to generate material for an upcoming record. The camp usually takes place in a spacious recording studio with a lot of separate rooms where writers can be divided into small groups.

In the 1990s camps were called "retreats." They were usually hosted and financed by an affluent publisher who had a castle here or a villa there, with the objective of cross-pollinating some of his/her writers with other creative souls to eat, drink and be…creative. There was not necessarily a particular project for which to write. It was loose, laid back and eclectic.

More recently, camps tend to target hot writers who have relationships with the gatekeepers of a project at hand. It should come as no surprise that in order to participate in a camp, one no longer has to be a seasoned pro who can flesh out a concept with one other collaborator. On the contrary, one must have a team spirit and be open to the idea of being randomly paired with another camper, or two, or three. If one has an arsenal of vibey ingredients to toss together with other campers' vibey ingredients (up against a sick beat or a cutting edge backing track), he or she is good to go.

Songwriting camps aren't my favorite venue. I'm definitely not on my best game in a pre-arranged setting where every song will be jockeying for position. It's a strange way to make art. However, all things considered, they *can* lead to a worthwhile song placement, which is why I haven't completely given them up.

I last participated in a camp in 2011. Most of the campers were provocatively dressed (if female), tattooed and hoodied (if male), friendly, enthusiastic, fun-loving, and competitive. They excelled in subject matter pertaining to partying, dancing and typically used the word "tonight" in a song title or as a theme. As if anything worth happening is going to happen *tonight!* Preferably while your hands are in the air. Labels couldn't get enough.

I arrived day one with a "when in Rome" attitude, in borderline age-inappropriate attire...purple satin bra straps falling off my shoulders, wobbling about on a pair of rarely worn stilettos, the thought being that if I located my inner party-girl maybe I could write one of those sexy cookie cutter smashes about going out and doing something naughty. (Tonight!)

I noticed there were some extraneous people hovering about and I wondered:

Who are these people? Counselors? Handlers? And why are they here? To steer their programmers toward the top topliners? To steer their topliners toward the top programmers? Are they that new breed of manager who micro-manages his/her clients' calendars? Who swap out one topliner for another at the last minute—as if they were interchangeable?

Well, I guess if you're clever enough to see an opportunity to carve a niche for yourself with creative people who would rather not be involved with keeping their own schedule, and if you have a flair for getting them "in the right room," fair enough and more power to you.

Hmm, maybe I need a handler. I feel so left out. I never needed one before. I open my iCal and tap something in. I delete when I have to reschedule. And if I have to reschedule, I apologize on my own behalf. I don't have someone do it for me–I'm a songwriter not a movie star.

There were other things going on at camp that I couldn't help but notice. Like...it helps to use a pseudonym instead of your real name. Something like "Magician" or "Aphrodisiac" is much cooler than Sophie Greenberg. So just for kicks, I asked to be called "Tapioca." I stayed in character as Tapioca the Topliner and wrote two songs in two days.

On the last night, all the campers convened for some catered fare. We shared wine, pasta, some unbelievable lasagna and…the titles of our freshly written songs. The first enthusiastic camper shouted, "Livin' Out Loud!," which was unfortunate, because *my* song was called "Lovin' Out Loud." See…we were all thinking inside the same box.

An aspiring Brit, who compared herself to the late, great Amy Winehouse, asked me who I was. Was I a manager? She must have observed I was twice anyone's age.

"No, I'm a camper actually," I replied.

"Oh really? Have you written anything I'd know?" she inquired. You're nobody unless somebody knows a song you wrote…but *if* you're a some-body, you *know* not to ask that question.

"Well, as a matter of fact, the Jessie J ballad, 'Who You Are.'" (Jessie was huge in the U.K. and I had to say *something* impressive.) "Oh and also," I couldn't help but add, "What-a-Girl-Wants-and-Bitch."

"Omagod, you're a legend!" she gasped! But her gasp had an "in that case what are you *doing* here?" shock and awe to it. It was a fair question. And my thought was, "I've been asking myself the same thing."

P.S. While we were busy chasing the "parties" and "tonights," soulful Adele, one of the biggest selling artists of her generation, proved she wasn't a fluke when her second album (and subsequently, a third) went Platinum. Ironically, she was anything but a party girl and, of course, labels became desperate for her clone.

Not too long after that, Lorde came along with her Goth look and minimalist production and blindsided us all with "Royals." "Royals" poked deliberate fun at all the talk of opulence and the braggadocious behavior in pop songs. Lorde might have put the kibosh on putting one's hands in the air once and for all, for soon after she mocked the overuse of the popular call-to-action, everyone lowered their arms.

As for clones, they will come and go and always be sought after no matter what, where or when. But an artist of real significance is never the same girl (or boy) twice.

1992. Miles Copeland hosted a retreat at his castle in the South of France. That's me next to Jud ("Run to You") Friedman with the infamous Phil Roy on his other side. Behind Jud is David ("Black Velvet") Tyson. No stilettos, bra straps or tattoos in sight.

Gleeful

ADAM ANDERS, THE Executive Music Producer for the blockbuster TV show "Glee," called me while I was in N.Y. with Layla over Spring Break and asked if I would be interested in writing an original song with him for the Season 2 finale of "Glee." Umm. Let me think. Okay! I was particularly enthusiastic because I knew I wouldn't be writing to a pre-existing backing track.

Adam told me a little bit about the episode in advance but I had fallen behind on the season, so I tried ordering up some Hulu on the flight home. The flight attendant informed me that the power ports had been disconnected due to a few "minor fires" (an oxymoron if I ever heard one). I tried watching on battery power, but the constant buffering drove me nuts. So when I got home, I pulled an all-night binge-watch. You can't go to a session like that without knowing what's been happening on the show. You just can't. You do *not* want to strike out.

I arrived at the studio the next morning with an idea. Peer Aström (Adam's writing partner) joined us via Skype from Sweden on a screen so large it felt like we were all in the room together. We wrote a song called "Pretending," as in, *how long can we, Rachel and Finn, aka Finchel, make believe we don't feel the way we do?* If you watched "Glee," you know the story.

Adam Anders and Peer Aström on Skype.

In general, television production schedules are tight. When it comes to the music there are usually a lot of hoops to jump through, cooks in kitchens, and standards-and-practices committees whose green light is essential. In this case, whatever we wrote would most likely be a go, not because Adam was Executive Music Producer, but because he knew what he was doing and the show's producers trusted him. I imagine that's *why* he was Executive Music Producer. We wouldn't have to compete, submit, and wait with bated breath for a thumbs-up. This concept was so foreign to me. Adam got a kick out of the way I kept checking in with him, week after week, to make sure our song was still in play…I just couldn't believe nothing would screw it up.

On the air date of the finale, I gathered my daughter, a few of her Gleek friends, and a few of *my* Gleek friends. We made popcorn, fired up the flat screen and the surround sound. The episode took place in N.Y.C.—The New Directions were performing at the Nationals:

After a season of confusion and romantic tension, Rachel and Finn confess their true feelings for each other. They emerge on stage from opposite wings and begin singing "Pretending"—*"Face to face/heart to heart/we're so close/yet so far apart."* They come together, they back away, they come together, they back away, and then, at an emotional peak, the music swells and whoosh…all the sound is muted. As the camera circles around them, in front of the huge audience in that auditorium, and in TV rooms across the country full of mothers and daughters just like us, Rachel and Finn kiss. It's about frickin' time.

Your heart is pounding. If a pin drops you won't hear it because the silence is that loud. Everything else can wait. You can pretend all you want, but when your lips touch…nothing is more real.

Layla and her young friends were imagining their future first kiss, (presumably they hadn't had one yet, but who knows), and the mommies were feeling nostalgic for theirs.

The following day "Pretending" was #7 on the iTunes Pop Chart. It wasn't a huge hit and the royalties didn't change my life. But here's the thing: Adam Anders could have called anyone in this town to write that song with him but he called *me*. So thank you, Adam Anders (and Peer). It was a highlight of my year to share such a *gleeful* moment with my daughter and our close friends, and to have written the song that was the prelude to…That Kiss.

Snapshot: Beautiful

I'm driving. I know that voice. It's Christina…
singing "Beautiful." I soften behind the wheel—like
butter at room temperature. This is what music is
supposed to do: *matter.* I'm inspired to hear a song
about believing in yourself—minus the cheddar.
(That's "SongwriterSpeak" for cheesy.) Those are the
hardest ones to write. I never get tired of this song.

Worst Session Ever

WHEN I FIRST started getting songs recorded, I'd brag. I'd see you at a party and I'd tell you how many songs I had coming out, before I'd ask how your ailing mother was. But, that was a *long* time ago and youth is an excuse for so much. I don't do that anymore. In fact, if you had dinner with me on a weekend, you might wonder what I did for a living. The subject of the music business might not even come up.

A few years ago, an up-and-coming, reportedly über-talented East Coast writer/producer was pursuing me. "Simon" sent me several emails suggesting we collaborate. And at the end of each one, he added a smiley face and a "hug" as a salutation. And links to past achievements. And a list of upcoming releases. They were quite impressive. I put him off for a while simply because his enthusiasm was a little too cute and uncomfortably enthusiastic for me.

On the other hand, you never know.

Maybe he's just really insecure as über-talented people often are. And, it is nice to be pursued. Maybe I shouldn't care so much about what he is or isn't if I want to get ahead. And I do.

Simon was coming to L.A. so we made a date to work, but lo and behold, he had to cancel. He sent an email that said he was being flown to an exotic location to work with someone *very* famous. "Who could say no to that? Big Hugs." I was being bumped by the guy I didn't want to work with in the first place.

As much as I wanted to cross Simon off my list of things to do, he began having huge success with high-profile artists and writing amazing songs I would have loved to have written with him. I put my distaste aside and agreed to have a coffee with him on my next trip to N.Y. so we could get to know each other a little better.

Maybe I'm totally wrong about him. I've misjudged people before.

Most of the time, I try not to work when I'm back East. I have a multitude of friends and family to catch up with. I thought Simon and I would just get that coffee. You know, a little kissing before we...but when he sent me his studio address, I realized he expected to get down to business that day. The misunderstanding could certainly have been mine. I apologized for the confusion and he graciously invited me to his home for some breakfast.

When I arrived, Simon seemed contemplative, aloof. Maybe he was annoyed that he had put the day aside to work and here we were wasting time over croissants. Whatever it was, he surely didn't seem like the guy who added smiley faces and hugs to electronic mail. I confided how much I missed N.Y. He reciprocated by mentioning his favorite lyricists.

"Breathe deeply," I told myself. It bothers me when a prospective partner goes on about past conquests, while *we're* supposed to be getting in the mood. Call me insecure; I do *not* consider that foreplay at all. I would never go on about Billy when I'm about to get into bed with Bobby.

But, now I was invested. We rescheduled a writing session for his next trip west. The upside, I reassured myself, was that Simon *was* a legitimate producer (no quotation marks needed) and there were fewer and fewer opportunities to get in a room with one and have proper *SongSex*. Whether we wrote a remarkable song or not remained to be seen, but at least I wouldn't be throwing sound bites up against sick beats. Of that, I was sure.

On the day Simon came to *my* home, things got even stranger. He wouldn't take any offerings. Coffee? Tea? Water? I noticed he had a little brown bag. That made me curious.

What's in that little brown bag? An apple? A Danish? A Trader Joe's turkey wrap? Didn't you think I'd provide snacks?

When I think back, I have to wonder if he didn't want to accept anything so that he wouldn't owe me anything later. Shortly after his arrival, he informed me that an artist he wanted to work with was coming to write with us. I had two thoughts:

1. *Couldn't you have run that by me first? That's a variable that entails a whole other headspace. I would have liked to prepare.*

2. *Great! Who is she?*

When "Victoria" arrived she did not look happy either. It seemed as if she didn't want to be there. Was it something I said? I hadn't even said *anything* yet. I found out that my suspicion was correct, because shortly after making introductions Simon announced he had to run down the hill for (I'm fairly sure it was) an audition to be an "American Idol" judge. I was left alone with Victoria and she said, "I don't want to be here." Wow. Apparently her label was putting pressure on her to work with other lyricists. I admired her candor. I just wished she had given it a second thought before saying something so thoughtless. Still, she was in my home. I ordered in some lunch.

When Simon returned he wasted no time. He strummed an eloquent chord progression on the acoustic guitar. He and Victoria were doing a lot of attention-paying to each other. When I'd suggest a line or a melody, there would be some acknowledgement, but that was about it. I couldn't put my finger on it but *something* was going on. What happened to the overly-eager overachiever who was dying to work with me? Maybe when Victoria came along, with her *big fat record deal*, I was an unnecessary third wheel. Part of me wished I was at a writing camp in a room with eight other Frankenwriters writing songs about what was going to happen "Tonight."

Painful as it was, a song got written. Ironically, it was quite beautiful. Yet the room was so cold. What did I expect? I'd had a feeling about him hadn't I? I kept telling myself, "you never know." But sometimes you know.

Victoria's manager stopped by. Simon whipped out a bio with a head-shot to make sure she, too, knew about all the projects he'd been working on and what he looks like in the best of lighting. Then, we had to move on from all the niceties because Simon needed to record Victoria's vocal. With her busy schedule, he might never get another chance. These are the producers a girl like me wants to work with, right? Players. The ones who get the job done!

Simon said he could set up anywhere—of course he could. With a laptop at one's fingertips, one doesn't need a full-on studio these days. In fact, traveling producers often bring all the essentials in one carry-on flight bag (Mary Poppins-style). I showed him into my office. He asked that I take some things off my desk. I cleared some space and excused myself. When I came back *all* my stuff (my phone, my lamp, my external hard drive, the framed picture of my father) was on the floor. At this point I was thinking…*whatever…I want this to be over. I need a cocktail.* With head-phones on and laser-like concentration, Simon hovered over his computer and programmed a divine bed of sound, something simple yet elegant, for Victoria to sing to. He would embellish the track in the weeks to come. What he created in fifteen minutes was extraordinary.

How on earth can such a detached human being compose such an inspired piece of music? Why can't he be as beautiful as his work?

He set up a mic. Victoria sang. She was intense and focused.

The girl can sing.

Before they left, Simon said he wished we had a bit of a chant or after-thought to add to the end of the hook. I sent him a few ideas the following week. He dismissed them all quite swiftly. The "Hugs" were now demoted to "Cheers." And there were no more Smiley Faces. :(

After the session, I was thinking, *WTF? That* was *so* bizarre. I sprayed my house with Lysol and tried to forget about it. A year later it all started making sense. My publisher called:

"Remember that song? The one you wrote with Simon and Victoria? Well, it's making the album and Simon says he'll give you 10%."

My response went something like this: "Umm…Excuse me? He can't give me something that's already mine. I own an equal share of everything I participate in. He can't take any of it away unless he asks. Nicely. And I would have to agree, which I don't. Plus…he should Man Up! Pick up the iPhone. Only a wimp would have his people call my people and tell them to call me."

I knew it wasn't my publisher's job to tell Simon where to go. She was only delivering a message to which I would determine the response. Still, I couldn't help but wish she had told him to call me himself. By agreeing to relay his message she was dignifying his arrogance.

I was up all night trying to figure out how people like Simon sleep. Ironically, they always seem to be the ones who do. After a few more weeks of unpleasantness from his advocates, I decided I didn't want to wake up to that toxic energy anymore. I offered them a tiny face-saving piece of my percentage, they took it, and the worst session ever was finally over.

IN RETROSPECT HERE'S how I see it: When Simon found out Victoria was available that day, he probably regretted scheduling me prior. Maybe she told him she wanted to work one-on-one with him—50/50. He was in a fix. He had canceled on me once. He couldn't blow me off again. Not to worry, he must have thought to himself; he'd deal with me later—a year later. And here we were. My assessment could very well be inaccurate. All I know is he had plenty of time to call and discuss the weirdness…and the song splits. But he didn't. Which doesn't surprise me because people in this business tend to disappear when things are about to get shady.

I wasn't the first songwriter to have this issue with Simon. There had been others…others who surrendered to the power of his awesomeness and went on to write *big fat hits* with him (and receive reduced percentages). I'm sure they would think I'm a fool. Maybe I am.

After this regrettable experience, I saw Simon at a small industry dinner party. The hostess requested the guests keep moving about the table so we'd all have a chance to connect. I wanted to get it over with. On a list of chores, always do the thing you dread the most first. I hated feeling bad about what happened. Surely there was a wee little olive branch I could extend. I moved toward an empty chair next to Simon.

"Hey Simon," I slithered into the chair. "You know, I really feel *bad* about what happened between us."

Not guilty, just Bad…and I mean about everything…the session, the phone call from my publisher, the emails from your lawyer.

"Yeah, it was weird that day," he murmured. *I'll say!* Then there was this awkward silence. Was that it? I wondered, isn't he going to say, "Yeah I *feel bad* too?" I didn't expect an apology. I wasn't trying to extract one. It just would have been nice to hear him say he felt something. Anything.

He *did* in fact manage to muster one more peculiar thought (under the circumstances.) He said he was sure our song would win a Grammy.

To be fair, I probably startled Simon by sneaking up on him. He didn't have a chance to compose himself. But if you ask me, I think we're from different planets. Over the course of time, I felt like I had witnessed an admiring compatriot morph into a self-serving wolf in sheep's clothing that operated on a sliding scale depending on how useful I could be in helping him further his agenda. Having said that, I had an agenda too, didn't I? There's no denying I found the guy somewhat off-putting from the get go, but still, out of a desire for success, I chose to collaborate with him anyway. So I guess I'm a bit of a wolf myself. Woof. The Universe doesn't look kindly upon that kind of insincerity, and thus, the train wreck.

In any event, the vocal Victoria sang in my office was the final vocal that appeared on her album. I know this because there was a little room "schmutz" (ambient noise) on the intro of our demo and it's there on the mastered recording too. So technically speaking, Simon, I could hit you up for a piece of the production fee since it was recorded at my house. I'll have my people call your people to let you know how much I want. How about 10%?

Hugs.

Farewell, My Muse

YOU REMEMBER JAKE, my unrequited college love? My muse? The one who would be the inspiration for so many songs to come? Even when I wasn't writing a song *about* him, if I was missing a line and had to find the hurt, I could tap into how I felt when I was *with* him. And voilà!

I'm grateful for Jake. Why? Because for a songwriter, a muse is a bottomless well of material from which to draw. I can turn one simple feeling this way and that, explore it from all angles, or tell the same story just a little differently and have a whole new song.

On the day we wrote "Almost Doesn't Count," for example, Guy played a wistful chord progression on the keyboard that transported me back to that Jake place, yet again. What about writing a song about a love that never quite "gets there?" I made a list of "almosts"…all the things that almost happened. Because, that's how I remember feeling…always on the verge. I gently laid my phrases into the cradle that Guy was rocking… *"Almost made you love me/Almost made you cry/Almost made you happy, Didn't I, Didn't I / Almost had me thinking you would turn around/But everybody knows, Almost doesn't count."*

You won't be surprised to know that over the years I was tempted to find Jake. I could say, "Hi, remember me? Just curious…why *didn't* you love me back?" Rejection-filled inquiries that still lingered in my songwriter heart. Even when we grow up, the part of a songwriter that resides in a state of arrested development remains handcuffed. We thrive on revisiting the unresolved.

I knew I was being silly. *I'm a grown woman, a mother; I love my husband. These are childish games.* However in 2010 with Google at my fingertips, my curiosity got the better of me. It was just too easy. With a couple of strokes and clicks I might finally get some answers.

So I did a little investigating, and with minimal surfing, Jake's name came up under a link to a website. I sat frozen with my thumb poised over the track pad, *one click away.*

I thought of the thousands of dreams I'd had of Jake in which I'd talk to him, but he couldn't hear me. Reach for him, but he couldn't see me. Of course, I knew those dreams were symbols of the unattainable; yearnings from another lifetime. Still, dreams are powerful. And in them, Jake was the same scruffy adorable nineteen-year old frat boy I remembered. Anything different wouldn't have made any sense. The part of me that was stuck in the past had no choice but to dream of him exactly as I left him. And for some irrational reason, that's what I expected to see when I clicked on the link.

Suddenly, there in a 2x2 square was a stranger, though my heart knew exactly who it was. People change. They get older. They get wider. Eyelids droop. But, the soul looking out from behind them? That stays exactly the same. The rest of him, I never would have recognized. He was puffy with thin hair. His nose had spread, his ears stuck out. He looked a little bit like…Shrek.

Shallow as it seems, right there in that nanosecond, as fast as it took me to fall for him so many years earlier, it was over. I didn't know it yet though. In fact, I had no idea until a few weeks later when the dreams stopped and when I went to "that place" for a line and came up empty. The world had moved on a long time ago and that JPEG finally pulled me forward with it. Broke the spell. The ghost that haunted me for years was sucked right out of my heart. I was horrified. What had I done? *Where will I go for that line? How will I ever be able to channel those feelings again?* I started wondering if I just should have left it alone. Farewell, my muse.

The Competition

IT WAS OPENING night of *Les Misérables* at Los Angeles's Ahmanson Theatre in downtown L.A. Layla and I were going with our mother/daughter friends Lisa and Holly. We had been waiting months for that night.

That afternoon Tom Mackay from Universal Records called to say that "Plan A," a song I wrote with Xandy Barry, was one of two original songs (out of hundreds) in contention for Javier Colon to sing on the final night of the first season of NBC's "The Voice." As per Tom's direction, we had been tweaking the production for weeks. Stripped down. Stripped up. More this. Less that. Xandy had been busting his ass chasing this one. Chris Mann, the third writer (who, ironically, would be a finalist on "The Voice" the following year), kept returning to the studio to re-sing the demo in all its incarnations. You do what you have to do to get the gig.

It was down to the wire. They were to make their decision the next day. First, however, Tom wanted me to get on the phone with Javier because *he* had some requests as well…ones that would make him feel more comfortable singing the song should it be chosen. I was down with that, except for one problem: I didn't want to be late for *Les Mis*. So I asked Tom if we could have that chat sooner rather than later.

I waited all day for the call, but it never came and finally we had to leave for the theatre. In my distraction I headed toward the Pantages in Hollywood instead of the Ahmanson. Layla was the one who realized we were in the wrong vicinity. She seized my iPhone and between its GPS and her excellent sense of direction, got us downtown without a minute (literally) to spare. We ran from the parking lot to the theatre doors. Lisa and Holly were waiting at the entrance. Inside, the audience was already seated. The lights were down. We shuffled our way to our seats trying carefully to step on as few toes as possible. Our butts were down for a total of about five seconds when the orchestra commenced, and the curtain went up, and, of course…my phone buzzed.

I slid it between my thighs and squeezed in order to hide the light and muffle the vibration until we were twelve minutes into the performance, at which time there was a scene change. Latecomers were allowed to enter the theatre, and those with small bladders were allowed to exit. I shuffled back down the aisle stepping on the same toes of the same irritated theatregoers, who, at this point, were even more displeased. I returned the call from the lobby. "Lars," an A&R consultant on "The Voice," said he wanted to put Javier on the line but as the contestants were sequestered, "*Could I stand by?*" They would call back momentarily. I waited. And waited some more. I went into the ladies' room and listened to "I Dreamed a Dream," (the song I looked forward the most to hearing) from a little speaker above the paper towel dispenser. Before I knew it, it was intermission.

I feared being trampled by the hundreds of ladies about to charge the ladies' room, so I left the building and resumed my waiting outside in the night air. After quite a long while the phone buzzed again. It was a four-way with Xandy, "Lars" and Javier. Javier made some reasonable requests. Could we go to the minor instead of the major? *Sure. That makes sense.* He gave us a line or two with which to build a bridge. *Ok with that.* Xandy would re-re-re-demo the song. Chris would re-re-re-sing and an mp3 would be sent to Tom by midnight.

I was able to shuffle back to my seat past the you-know-whos, in time for the last musical number and the standing ovation. So much for opening night.

In the end, we didn't get the gig. At least Tom had the courtesy to call and let me know, not just send an email, or a text. They chose another song written by my esteemed colleague, Lindy ("Stitch by Stitch") Robbins, which I have to say (I'm sorry Lindy), I never even heard, because at that point, I needed to take a break from "The Voice."

Three seasons later Judith Hill sang an insane rendition of "What a Girl Wants" for her "Voice" blind audition. I was in London at the time. My phone lit up with notifications. I watched her performance on YouTube. She was amazing. I reset my DVR; "The Voice" is back in the queue.

Me, Javier, Xandy.

P.S. Layla, Lisa, Holly and I saw Les Misérables *(the movie) when it opened on Christmas Day 2012. Anne Hathaway's moving performance of "I Dreamed a Dream" made up for my having to listen to it in the ladies' room from the speaker above the paper towels.*

Snapshot: Human

Rewind. My daughter thinks she is introducing me to "Human" by the Killers. Little does she know I am already obsessed with the song. "Are we human or are we dancer?" Or it might be *denser*. Whatever *that* means. It doesn't matter. He is leaving somewhere and searching for something else. He is looking for the answer. And so am I. I am right there with him.

He Ain't Heavy

A FEW MONTHS after we started dating, Adam and I were lolling about in a swimming pool, my back to his chest. He was keeping me afloat with his arms locked underneath mine, the back of my head resting on his shoulder. He had me completely buoyed, my limbs dangling lazily in the water. We decided we'd call this the state of being *totaled*...when one gives up total control and accepts the other's support. We could of course switch places in which case *Adam* would be *totaled*. Either way we liked the idea that one could trust the other to be in charge, while the other surrendered. We agreed we'd do this for each other even when we weren't in water.

Shortly after our status changed from "long distance relationship" to "cohabiting," but *before* we were officially married, we formed a corporation and called it "Totalled, Inc." It didn't have much of a ring to it, but it was the meaning behind the name that mattered. We inadvertently spelled it wrong and on occasion, we've received a check in the mail that can't be deposited because the issuer spelled "Totaled" correctly. (Doesn't that look wrong to you? It does to me.)

Since that day in the pool, Adam and I have been *totalling* each other... alternating positions (the *totallee* and the *totaller*) depending on who could use the solace and who was feeling strong. If a director didn't send Adam notes on a cue until a day before "the mix," and he had to pull an all-nighter, I *totalled* him. When I was sure I was becoming invisible and might never work another day, he'd order out and put in a wash, while I sulked and took an extended time-out. He *totalled* me. You had to be patient until the *totallee* recovered, wait your turn if you needed to crash, because it went without saying, especially with a baby on-board, that only one of us could decompress at a time.

It's been a blessing to be granted the space, the indulgence, the escape from the insanity of this unrelenting, ever humbling, though sometimes glorious business we both navigate. A comfort to know everything wouldn't fall apart if (when) we did so individually. I'm pretty sure that's a *glue* we couldn't have survived without.

Wedding day.

Get Off My Cloud

DURING ONE OF those writing camps I swore I'd never participate in again, I wrote a song with fellow camper Rob Wells for Katharine McPhee. It was called "Note 2 Self." My staunch supporter Teresa, Katharine's A&R representative, had extended an invitation to me, even though she was aware that camps weren't my cup of tea. Still, she wanted to give me the choice. Of course, I went—one last time.

I loved how the song turned out. Thing is, there are dozens of songs written over the course of a camp and there's only room for a certain amount on a traditional album. It's like musical chairs, except there are so many more songs than there are chairs.

Months passed with no word as to whether we made the cut. So I checked in with Teresa. She texted back, "Everyone at the label loves 'Note 2 Self'…interesting thing though…it got leaked on YouTube!" "Really?" I was surprised. "How? The only people that have it are you, Rob, Katharine and I."

I checked YouTube to see what was up. Indeed, there it was. How did it get there? Was Teresa suspicious of me? Of Rob? Some writers leak their own songs to try to get a buzz going, because if they're successful, the label could be swayed into releasing it commercially. I'm not that brave. There are so many things that could backfire…like what if they decided *not* to include it on the record *because* it's been pre-exposed? In which case, it would still be out there with Katharine's name, voice and photo attached and these days no other artist would ever get near it.[1]

Wait. Maybe Katharine leaked it herself. *She* wanted to create a little buzz of her own. Or…maybe it was Teresa! How clever. Katharine had been busy filming "Smash" and there'd been so little time to record. Maybe *Teresa* wanted to make sure "Katharine the recording artist" remained in the spotlight. As if I wasn't paranoid enough, I also considered the possibility that someone from the writing camp got their hands on a copy and made it public, because if *my* song were exposed, *theirs* would have better shot at "finding a chair." I was beside myself. (Adam says I'm a conspiracy theorist. I can't imagine what he's talking about.)

When I calmed down I came to my senses: the writer was *undoubtedly* an obsessive fan who got his kicks from digging up something off limits and distributing it to other undernourished fans. It's an unstoppable epidemic in a world where you don't have to be an experienced hacker to make a real nuisance of yourself.

I called Rob because I knew he'd know how to get to the bottom of it. He was aghast. He did some fine Internet detective work and found a chat in which the "chatter" had asked the "uploader" ("Kyle") how he came upon the song. Kyle replied that he already knew the *name* of the song (possibly from something Katharine tweeted) and that a few months ago he Googled it along with "Katharine McPhee" and ta da…a link took him to a "Note 2 Self" MP3 on somebody's SoundCloud.

Really? I use SoundCloud; when I need to send a few songs to someone, I upload them to the site and share the link. Come to think of it, I might have uploaded "Note 2 Self" on *my* SoundCloud a few months ago (when I wanted to send the finished mix to Teresa), and I *was* having trouble figuring out how to make my tracks private. I had even contacted SoundCloud Help because I was so confused.

---

[1] Sometimes a singer posts a song on YouTube for which they were hired to sing the demo. If that song is about to be released by a superstar, labels go berserk. A debut song, beaten to the punch by a WannaBe can take the wind out of the sails of any release. Sometimes the label pays that demo singer a considerable sum to un-post their version. Sometimes the singer takes the money and then re-posts it after the release.

I had a horrible feeling in my stomach. I leaked my own song. Inadvertently—indirectly—but I did. For all intents and purposes, I put some bait on a hook and attracted a fish. What a dork! Admittedly, I am not a file-sharing aficionado. I surely didn't realize how easy it was for someone to walk onto your cloud and download your songs, and then upload them elsewhere without your permission.

Rob filed infringement notices with YouTube insisting they remove the song from the site. I canceled my SoundCloud account; they never responded to my inquiry and even if they had, I was too frustrated with them for making it so complicated! There are many other user-friendly, private-only, file-sharing sites. I made a "Note 2 Self" to find one.

And so, Teresa, Katharine and Rob (Rob especially, to whom I haven't had the courage to come clean), if you're reading this, I humbly apologize.

Katharine McPhee and me.

P.S. I have since gotten re-acquainted with SoundCloud. Not surprisingly they have user-friendly privacy settings. I must not have been implementing them correctly. So all my confusion admittedly was, umm…user error. My apologies to you too, SoundCloud.

Fucking You

IT WAS VALENTINE'S Day. I walked into a session and asked my dry-witted collaborator, Aimee Proal, how many songwriters she thought were writing a song called "Valentine's Day." And she said, "Yeah, I know what you mean. We should write a song called, 'Fuck Love.'" And so we did.

When Layla was younger, I tried to keep her from tweezing her eyebrows, talking to strangers, and R-rated pop songs. I know that's hypocritical coming from a woman who tweezes her eyebrows, befriends strangers, and wrote a song called "Bitch." But let's face it; the word "Bitch" is mild compared to some of the lyrics in pop music today. Shocking is in. And if you keep shocking the listener, he or she becomes desensitized. Immune even. If they want to be noticed, artists have to keep pushing the envelope to come up with something brazenly outrageous. They have to ask themselves what they're willing to say to stay in the game. (As a songwriter, I have to ask myself what *I'm* willing to say as well.)

For example, in 2010's "What's My Name" Rihanna sings "*I wanna see if you can go downtown on a girl like me.*" I'm not sure I understand how she could ask him to do a certain deed when he doesn't even know what her name is. Be that as it may, Layla was twelve when the song was all the rage and when we heard it in the car, my maternal reflexes had me muting that particular passage.

Nevertheless, I'll always be a fan of Rihanna because when Layla and I had the good fortune of being invited to one of her rehearsals, she told Layla she had beautiful eyebrows and Layla stopped tweezing—for at least a week. These things matter to a mother. Plus, Rhi-Rhi balanced out her hyper-sexuality with the tender and brutally vulnerable, "Love the Way You Lie." I turned the radio up.

SOME YEARS AGO, I went to Florida with "Tony B.," Enrique Iglesias' music director, to work with the superstar for his new record. Enrique's record label wanted a *big fat hit*—a "Grammy contender." (If you know the secret recipe for those, do tell.) Enrique had been smart. His father had banked his career on crooning romantic ballads and Enrique was doing a good job following suit. He was coming off of the super successful "Hero" and "Addicted." Mainstream material; stuff he could count on.

It wasn't easy keeping the fun-loving Enrique's attention. No sooner would he be enthusiastic about an idea, than he would laugh it off an hour later. He kept interrupting our attempts at creating a Grammy contender to demonstrate his new Segway or show us how he put his dog on the treadmill for a workout. We took frequent breaks for meals, once with his girlfriend, tennis star Anna Kournikova (that was worth taking a break for), but in essence, nothing was getting done. Needless to say, Tony B. and I wanted to get at least one song in the can before we flew back home.

So, on our last night we did something naughty: We decided to "pre-write" a whole song in the privacy of my hotel room. We would make sure it was an undeniable hit (in our humble opinions) and the next day, we'd present it as if it were unfolding for the first time while we were "writing" it with Enrique. We'd have to be very careful not to get found out from a look or a snicker between us that could give us away. It was unethical and disingenuous to say the least, but we were running out of options.

The song we pre-wrote, "Driving You Home," followed the formula. It was sexy and romantic and if I were the girl to whom Enrique was singing, I'd have shagged him right there in the front seat, or the back seat, or on top of the car. Enrique seemed really into it. He recorded vocals. Then, the next day he laughed that song off too. (Served us right.) Maybe he was confused or maybe he just wasn't sure in which direction he wanted to go.

He surely figured it out though, because two albums later he released a single called, "I Like It," an audacious booty shout-out to a prospective hook-up in which he unabashedly sang about what he was going to do to her while both of their significant others were out of town, and what she would say about it ("I Like It"). He followed that up with the arrogant, super-hooky and anything but subtle, "Tonight (I'm Fuckin' You)." The original title was "Tonight (I'm Lovin' You)," but radio wanted an "explicit" version for the masses, so you might have heard "Lovin' You" on Lite FM but "Fuckin' You" was everywhere else. Both singles went through the roof.

Like it or not, egotism, rudeness, and the glorification of bad behavior are themes that resonate all too well with much of today's mainstream music-buying demographic. So, artists (and songwriters) have the right to give the fans what they want. I get it. Plus…you can't be deep and meaningful *all* the time. Personally, I wouldn't mind hearing a little more Ray LaMontagne. But it doesn't matter what I think, because there goes Enrique now…on the way to Wells Fargo…and I'm pretty sure he's laughing his ass off.

The Way It Wasn't

I WAS TALKING with two millennial songwriter pals. We always seem to get into spirited discussions about how the business has changed. They like to hear my stories. It reminds me of how my mother used to tell me about "the olden days." The business was never easy. Now it's even harder. I'm nostalgic for when it was just hard.

My two young pals were grumbling because a certain A&R exec didn't respond with feedback on a song he had specifically asked them to write. I told them that back in the day, even when a song was passed on we'd get a formal letter saying "Thank you for your submission, but we feel that your song sucks because...(fill in the blank)." At least you felt like you existed... that you weren't just releasing songs blindly into the abyss. My pals were intrigued.

To be fair to twenty-first century A&R execs (the ones who still have jobs), today you can take one song and email it to fifty of them with the tap of a fingertip, or transmit a whole playlist via Dropbox. So, if one hundred writers do that every day, how can A&R realistically respond to *all* of them?

When I was coming up, we had to go to a cassette duplicating service and make copies of our song. Then we'd affix a label to each cassette, put one in a padded jiffy bag with a lyric sheet and a cover letter...address it, staple it shut, weigh it, stamp it, drop it in the mailbox and wait. Talk about snail mail. So maybe they got one hundred submissions a *month*. In which case, they had time to actually listen and respond, even if the response was a stock letter dispatched by an intern. Not that I *ever* wish to go back to these methods. But there was just more reciprocation *and* appreciation. A&R execs *wanted* to receive songs. They were looking for them. Without good songs, they couldn't make good records.

My pals looked at me like I was Wilma Flintstone. It was the same face I made when my parents told me, "once upon a time TV had no color." The same face Layla makes when I tell her you had to get up off the couch to change the channel, or adjust the volume, crank open your car window, wait a week to see a picture you took, refer to a road map, call back if you got a busy signal.

My young friends don't know life without Bluetooth and Wi-Fi. Still, I hope that in the future, they will live to tell their own generational tales to *their* songwriting descendants. That is if they can survive in the business long enough. And here's why they may not be able to....

- *The Way It Was…was*: if you wrote a whole song that was included on an album as an "album track"—never released as a single—and that album went Platinum (sold a million copies), you could have earned $91,000 in income (with the statutory rate at 9.1 cents per track on an album). It wasn't uncommon for an album to *sell* a million copies. One or two of those every year? You were in good shape.

- *The Way It Is…is*: you can have twenty album tracks placed on twenty different albums in the course of a year, but you might not even earn $5,000, because albums aren't selling. Albums aren't selling because a single or favorite track can be purchased (or accessed— see next Chapter) on its own. So why buy the whole album? For many music *fans*, this is not a bad thing, but the fact remains that it has severely eaten away at a songwriter's ability to make a living. While it is *possible* to land a huge single and win the lottery (a prize that could be in excess of a million dollars), there are precious few winning tickets to be had.

- *Plus*…the playing field is a lot wider. One no longer has to know how to play an instrument or construct an entire lyric in order to enter "songwriter" as his/her occupation on his/her income tax form. Computer programming or a smartphone songwriting app can go a long way. Fewer records being sold? More writers? Do the math.

- *Plus*…as we have seen, since songwriting sessions have turned into more of a group sport, there may be eight collaborators instead of two, so everybody gets a smaller share.

- *And*…since job security at record labels has become an oxymoron and profits across the board have diminished, it seems like even label execs have their eye on songwriting royalties and how they can wrangle a piece of that pie for themselves. Everywhere I turn, there's somebody coming at me with a fork. It's not unusual to see people listed on label copy who weren't even in the room when the song was conceived. The A&R person for instance—the artist, the producer's protégé, an invisible friend, somebody's hamster.

- *Plus*…some A&R execs are signing and managing their own stable of writers, or doing joint ventures with publishing companies, so who do you think they will go to when they need a song?

- *Plus*…writers and producers are signing *their* own protégés to *their own* companies. So, it's not unusual for there to be more than one company in succession accounting to a songwriter (trickle-down publishing), making for a longer pipeline and more and more forks taking pieces of pieces of pie!

It's the Wild West out there.

Given these conditions, what are the chances that a budding serial songwriter will be able to buy an engagement ring, pay a mortgage, have a baby, put a couple of kids through school?

Nobody likes to talk about it, because anyone who's been in it as long as I have is afraid of being thought of as a Flintstone. *And*…as I've mentioned before, anyone who's *new* to the business doesn't know it to be any different. It's all status quo to them.

There are still songs written in full by independent songwriters that get recorded simply because they're *that* good and they're in the right place at the right time, and the writer isn't forced to distribute pieces of what's rightly his or hers. But, it doesn't happen often enough.

I've learned to keep things in perspective, though. For one, I was in my heyday when the champagne was flowing and CDs were flying off the shelves. I will never have to wonder what it was like when business was booming. More importantly, I do not have a terminal disease; I am not broke, hungry or unloved. I don't suffer from depression. My family is healthy. I am quite aware I am living a charmed life and should it end tomorrow, while abbreviated, I would have to say my life was full and rich, and happy. I appreciate that the advance of modern technology is inevitable, necessary and beneficial, and I'm certainly aware that changing business models are forcing millions of people out of work all over the world, not just serial songwriters.

But let's face it: regardless of changing business models, if you're in a *youth*-driven business, at some point you're *going to start to feel pushed out.* Sooner or later you're going to wonder if it's time to pass the baton to a new generation.

(Not So) Gently Down the Stream

BY 2010, a new technology that would further challenge the already dubious proposition of making a living as a songwriter was gaining momentum— *digital streaming.*

Streaming offered consumers instant access to a myriad of songs. Instead of downloading them or owning a physical copy, they could listen to whatever they wanted, whenever they wanted, as many times as they wanted for as little as…nothing. It was, still is, practical, convenient, immediate, and versatile. It allows the user to share playlists and discover new artists he or she might not have discovered otherwise. For the music enthusiast (myself included), it's the best thing that ever happened. For the songwriter (myself included), it's potentially disastrous.

Here's why: In the 1940s, laws were put into place that determined the rates at which songwriters were paid when their music was played on established platforms—traditional radio for instance. Back then no one could have imagined a *digital* age. But seventy years later there it was, and music streaming services were able to apply those outdated laws in order to justify paying songwriters rates that were alarmingly below fair market value. No one did anything illegal, but, sadly, these laws remain in force, and digital music services have become multi-billion-dollar corporations on the backs of the very people who make it possible for them to exist in the first place— the songwriters who create the only product that they offer: *songs.*

To add insult to injury, record labels were not constrained by the same government regulations and were able to negotiate *their* terms with the streaming companies in a free market environment. As a result, labels were able to negotiate a much higher royalty rate for the right to stream their *recordings* than songwriters receive for the right to stream their *songs*.

While it is still *possible* for a songwriter to earn a healthy performance royalty for a mid-charting single that gets played on terrestrial radio, *or* a substantial payday for a *huge* hit, the vast majority of us do not generate singles every day, if ever. And make no mistake: streaming is here to stay and it's going to continue to replace existing formats that still generate dependable income from *any* type of song.

To put things in perspective, songwriter Linda Perry reported earning a mere $350 for 12 million streams of her song "Beautiful"—and you *know* how I feel about "Beautiful." Lucky for Linda, *she* has a diverse financial portfolio. But it's still not just. And for the newcomer, or the majority of writers who are simply trying to make ends meet, these outrageously low streaming rates are making life financially unsustainable.

Songwriters and their allies have begun emphatically making the case for why the government needs to review the "consent decrees" that were put into effect during World War II. Here are some of the arguments:

- Although one would think the ability to stream unlimited music anyplace, anytime, anywhere should have *increased* compensation, songwriters are unable to negotiate a fair market rate for their work. No other American business has their pay rate set by the government.

- If we are forced to accept these low rates, many of us will have to give up the profession; that song you love, that you might dance to at your wedding or lull your baby to sleep with, may never get written.

- Technological progress has surpassed the legal structure governing the economics of our industry. It's time Congress updated laws that were written over seventy years ago.

There are rebuttals to these arguments and respectively, the narratives go like this:

- All of the exposure from streamed music gives artists and songs invaluable free publicity, which could lead to further opportunity and revenue.

- There will always be songwriters who *can and will* stick it out no matter what.

- Technology puts talented passionate people out of work every day. They should buck up, adjust and find another source of income.

Of course, I have rebuttals to these rebuttals: The argument for free publicity can be made for any goods or services. And yes, people *will* always write songs, but under current conditions, the diverse middle class of the profession will fade into memory.

There is one argument however, for which I have not heard a counter view: the consumption of streamed music is generating *massive* amounts of revenue. The problem is almost *all* of it is winding up in someone else's bank account. And if *you're* going to build *your* fortune from *songwriters' songs,* why should *songwriters* have to find another job?

What on Earth Is a Hit Song?

I WISH I knew. If I had the answer I would have written a whole lot more.

Anybody who tells you there's a formula…like always have the title in the first line of the hook or always get to the chorus in thirty-seven seconds, is probably describing a winning scenario that works sometimes, but I assure you, no formula will work every time. As for me, as soon as I think I've found the perfect cocktail, somebody hides my vodka.

Having said that…I have picked up some songwriting tips from partners and colleagues that have resonated with me over the years. Such as…

- **Stay True**

  I was on a songwriting panel with Kara ("American Idol") DioGuardi, and she said something that was quite matter-of-fact. Let me Karaphrase: "If it doesn't feel inspired going in, it won't feel inspired coming out." Sometimes the simplest ideas go under-appreciated. How many times have I been complicit in finishing a song I wasn't "feeling," so as not to be the stick-in-the-mud or disappoint my co-writer? The answer is: a lot more than I'd like to admit. Even though sometimes those songs manage to get recorded, more often than not, they don't, and then I fail with something I didn't believe in in the first place.

- **Walk Away**

  When you're stuck...take a walk! This can be more visually stimulating in a city; however, there are other ways to clear your head. Here in L.A., we drive to a place where we can walk. Or we sit by a pool; there are so many pools.

- **Separate**

  Dan James, Leah Haywood and I had bits and pieces of a puzzle that we just couldn't seem to put together. Dan left the studio for a coffee and a smoke and as soon as he came back in, he spewed a whole hook. Just like that—as effortless as a fart. After all that constipation, Leah and I looked at each other—WTF, Dan? And... did somebody get that?

  Songwriter Michelle Lewis excuses herself to "powder her nose." She always comes back with a clever line; I know it has nothing to do with her nose. She just needs a little space.

- **Double Down**

  When I first worked with Albert Hammond, Sr., he suggested using the same exact line back to back. I said, "Albert...Umm...you just used that line." And he said, "So what? Did it feel good?" It did. He said, "Then don't worry."

- **Be Ready**

  Though your mobile device with its Voice Memo App is most likely by your side 24/7, sometimes it's just nice to feel a pen glide around on paper. So keep a pad of Post-it notes on the piano, under your pillow, in your closet, in your sock drawer, in the spice cabinet, by your toothbrush, the kitchen sink, in your man-purse, the glove compartment, the bathroom, your gym locker—you get the idea—because you never know when an idea is going to tap you on the shoulder. You can swear you'll remember it, but you won't.

- **Work It Out**

  Get that blood closer to your brain. Good things happen when your heart beats faster.

- **Leave Room to Pace**

  Get out from behind the computer. Staring at a screen can hold you hostage. Release yourself. Your mind is freer when it's not confined.

- **Keep Going…**

  …even when you feel like you're filling up pages with meaningless gibberish. Often the golden nugget turns up at the very end of the last page of the stuff you thought was nonsense.

- **Be Disciplined**

  Sit at the piano or with that guitar every morning and noodle… even if nothing comes. Eventually something will.

- **Word Games**

  Crossword puzzles let you practice fitting words into limited or specific spaces…twisting and turning concepts around until something clicks—like writing lyrics. Sometimes, just when you're certain you can go no further, the next day you'll be crossing the street and voilà…23 Across (or that missing line) becomes obvious. Your brain is working, even when you're not.

- **Listen**

  Keep your ears open for snippets of conversation that catch your attention—a slur from a drunk in the checkout line, a blurb about the weather on the news, a lament from a tired two-year-old. We hear things selectively for a reason.

- **Rhyming**

  Soft rhymes or sound-alikes are pleasing. They have texture. They are fresh. Exact rhymes can sound stale. A perfect rhyme that's "ballpark" is not nearly as interesting as a scrappy one that tells the truth.

- **The More the Merrier**

  If you can't sing, consider writing with someone who can, especially if you are aiming to pitch the song to an artist with a big voice. A singer with range can take you to melodic places you wouldn't have ventured yourself, simply because…you can't sing!

- **Access Your Madness**

  Even the most mentally healthy songwriter harbors a bit of emotional dysfunction. This is no time to be sensible. Unleash it. It will serve you well.

- **Dream It**

  When you're searching for an elusive word or an alternative melodic shape, concentrate on it when you go to bed. What we fall asleep thinking about is often what we dream about. If it comes to you in your sleep, document it as soon as you wake up, because we forget 90% of our dreams within ten minutes of waking. It's been said that the introduction to "Satisfaction" came to Keith Richards in a dream. Makes me want to take a nap. Yawn.

- **Set the Mood**

  If you want a song to have a certain melancholy feel, listen to another song that has a similar melancholy feel, while you're working on the new song. I'm not suggesting you rip it off...but use it like Viagra, if you will, to get in the mood. (If you remain inspired for more than four hours, be sure to get medical help right away.)

- **Keep Perspective**

  I'm uncomfortable when a co-writer automatically defers to me. He might think I know better just because I once wrote a big hit. I don't. Conversely, sometimes I'm writing with someone who just had a hit and I start thinking maybe *she* knows better. She doesn't.

- **Stay Clear**

  A lot of great songs have been written under the influence, but be careful. While being high may open your mind and let you see things in a different light, sometimes that heady mist of open-mindedness makes it hard to tell whether you're really brilliant or just imagining you are. See "The Opportunists" (page 45).

My apologies to everyone who saw the title of this chapter and thought by reading it they'd know how to write a hit song. It's just not that simple. If I *had* to come up with one X factor that I could cite as a characteristic most hit songs have in common (and this excludes hit songs that are put forth by an already well-oiled machine…that is, a recording artist who has so much notoriety and momentum that just about anything he or she releases, as long as it's "pretty good," will have a decent shot at succeeding), I would say it would be: *A universal sentiment in a unique frame.*

Good luck.

Ain't Gonna Happen

A MANAGER OF an aspiring artist (henceforth called GeeGee) asked me to "doctor" one of her songs. This means I would take a song with improvable lyrics and improve them. This particular song, "Ain't Gonna Happen," was co-written by GeeGee and, umm, her A&R point person. I would think that writing a song with your A&R point person puts you in a favorable position at the label. (It might also be why you need help with your lyric.)

To get a vibe on an artist, I usually check to see if they've posted anything on YouTube. They *always* have. I found a video called, "Stick 'Em Up." It was filled with carefree girls in wet cut-offs, washing cars and shooting each other with oversized water guns. The water was white and creamy. In all the still images online, GeeGee had her tongue out or her eyes crossed.

"Ain't Gonna Happen" was far more mild than "Stick 'Em Up." Sort of Ke$ha-lite. Apparently they were going for a bit of an image adjustment. In any case, I wasn't *that* excited about meeting GeeGee. I didn't think we'd have that much in common, but I *did* think the song had potential. Plus, she *was* writing with her A&R exec. So, chances were it had a shot.

I rescheduled another session to accommodate her. I confirmed place and time with her manager (Malibu, at 11:00am), but the morning of the meeting I received an email from him saying "GeeGee needs to move the meeting to noon...and to Hollywood." *No biggie...that's actually more convenient for me.* I was about to walk out the door at 11:30, when I got a call saying that now GeeGee had to move the meeting to 3. *Seriously? Do they think I have no life?* I bit my tongue. *I have been dealing with this kind of inconsideration for years. It will never change.*

So I worked on the lyric for a few *more* hours. And then, buzz, buzz: What's this? A screenshot of a dropped pin on a Google Map: yet another updated meeting place—the "Veggie Grill" on Westwood Blvd. Back to the West Side? The map had originated with GeeGee and the manager's *assistant* had forwarded it to me. (I noticed *the manager* had extricated himself from the commotion. I mean communication. No, I mean commotion.) Manager's assistant followed up with another text: "This is the last change and GeeGee promises to be there by 3:30 the *latest.*"

WTF? What happened to 3? What happened to 11? What happened to Hollywood? I feel like a ping-pong ball. If any of my recent records had been released as singles, like I was "promised," I would blow this off and go to the mall.

But they weren't. So I was off to Westwood.

You're as big as your last hit and it's been a few years. Shit. I'm gonna wind up creeping back up the canyon in rush hour.

I thought about what my friend Bennett Kaufman said to me a week before: "It's a numbers game. You never know when your 'last hit' is gonna happen next." Touché, Bennett.

I was ten minutes early. I hated myself for that. GeeGee wasn't there yet. Shocking. *I'll just get a cuppa coffee and wait for her.* But the Veggie Grill didn't *sell* coffee.

What? Fine. I'll have an iced tea. I don't even like iced tea. But holding one will make it appear like I am doing something besides waiting.

3:30. *I'll wait ten more minutes. There's got to be a reason for this waste of a day.*

4:00. *I'm Leaving. Even if our paths cross in the doorway, I'm not turning around.*

En route back home the assistant called: "GeeGee screwed up. She feels terrible. She's actually waiting for you at the Veggie Grill on Santa Monica Boulevard" (right around the corner from the one on Westwood Boulevard). *Of course she is!* Obviously, the Universe was testing me. The definition of crazy is doing the same thing over and over again and expecting a different result.

Do I go? I have the time. That's not the question. Do I have any self respect is the question. On the other hand, I am having a fantastic hair day and no one is getting to see what I look like.

That alone was reason enough to reconsider. Then I thought about the video and the white creamy spray from the water guns and the wet cut offs and the tongue and the crossed eyes. And all of a sudden, I was driving up Coldwater Canyon blissfully heading towards home sweet home.

I'm not stupid...I didn't forget about what Bennett said about the numbers game. The song at hand was called, "Ain't Gonna Happen." Ironically, maybe it will...it could. And *that* is what keeps a serial song-writer going on these wild goose chases.

Maybe I'm just exhausted and tomorrow I will have my sense of humor back. If that's the case and the manager calls (or the manager's assistant) to reschedule, GeeGee will have to come to my house. And I'll tell her what time.

P.S. And if they like my revisions, and if the song is released and sees the light of day, you'll never read this. But you're reading it, so you know what never happened.

Suddenly

SOMETIMES I HEAR Simon and Garfunkel singing, "Slow down you move too fast." They're in a little bubble following me around as I scurry about my day. They're in my underwear drawer as I hurry to get dressed. They're in my coffee cup as I grab it to go. Those two heavenly voices; they sing extra loud when I'm multitasking. And I usually am.

See, I get caught up with work. I don't turn things down. I take a meeting and listen to lip service from the A&R exec who says he thinks my song is perfect, but I know he will ultimately use the one from a writer of whom he gets a piece. I get angry with myself when someone's album is finished and I didn't try hard enough to get a song on it. I go to a writing camp to try to raise my batting average, even though there's a decent chance the artist we are rallying around may be dropped. I often have a choice to make: write yet another song or go to lunch with the girls. I usually write another song.

Recently, things changed. I had had a tiny bump on my breast for years. It was barely noticeable and I had been assured it was nothing and would never turn into something. I'd been so busy, that I barely noticed it was getting bigger. So I went to my doctor. The second he touched it he said, "I don't like this"…and that's when things suddenly started to seem surreal. I thought about how my life might slip away from me in the next few months. I'd have to put everything on hold at least until I could find out just how much life I had left.

He didn't waste any time. He made some appointments for later on in the day. It was a Friday. He didn't want to "have to wait out the weekend" to see what "we were up against." I liked how he said "we" even though it was actually just me!

I had a mammogram and then I waited in the waiting room for the ultrasound, no appetite for the first time in years. I flipped through magazines full of airbrushed PerfectGirls with PerfectTits, healthy recipes that could "put years on my life," anti-aging creams that could take years off. And there was Christina Applegate, that year's breast cancer Prom Queen staring back at me. What a SexySurvivor. I felt guilty for all the walks I sponsored, but never actually walked in.

Amazing, the things that seemed trivial. Car dents, cavities, song splits, bunions, cellulite, writer's block, that spinning pinwheel on my computer screen, facial hair, aging, A&R execs who manage writers, stopped-up toilets, the falling out I had with Simon, the falling out I had with Jeff, a few other falling-outs, albums not selling, streaming income, the constant rotation of Jack and Diane. I made promises to myself and deals with a God I'm not sure I believed in: if I get to live, I'll heed Paul and Art. I'll drink green tea (yuk), do yoga (yawn). I'll slow the fuck down.

The radiologist took me in to the examining room. I was on the alert for a widening of his eyes. He swirled the ultrasound probe over the bump and then he said, "I don't think this is anything to worry about." He elaborated, but I didn't hear anything else. As suddenly as my life flashed before my eyes hours earlier, it just as suddenly resumed.

I've never taken things for granted. My friends will tell you that I'm always professing how lucky I am...about all the blessings bestowed upon me. Along with my losses, I've had an abundance of wins and just the fact that I was conceived at all—that that one particular sperm merged with that one egg—is a miracle. I could so easily have been someone else if my father (or my mother) had coughed. I say this all the time. So it's not like I'm a boor who doesn't appreciate the improbability of existence...who isn't aware that I am merely dust in the wind. Here I am. I passed Go and collected two hundred dollars.

But this experience was a wake-up call on a whole different level. I decided I wasn't going to nag Adam to call the contractor about fixing the Jacuzzi pipe that he, the contractor, had broken. My husband hates confrontation and it's just not worth ragging on him to do it. I'm going to forget about telling my daughter to clean her room and instead just be grateful to have an untidy, imperfectly wonderful family. I'm outside in the soft shade eating watermelon, so slowed down I'm almost stalled. Do you hear me Paul and Art? I'm having a moment of self-reflection. Tomorrow, I'll sip green tea while that lyric waits. And I'll even consider some downward dog.

Grammy Fever

IT'S FEBRUARY 2013—GRAMMY week is nuts. There's been a party every night since Monday. There's another one tonight on the Paramount Lot—the "Friends and Family" party, which is basically everyone in the music business. Seriously, there will be at least ten thousand people there—VIPs and WannaBes. This party is *so* big, if you want to sit it out, you can tell everyone you went and they will never know you didn't. Every year I say, *this* year I'm not going. I always end up changing my mind. As soon as I get there, all I can think about is my pajamas. I walk around with a small bottle of water and tell everyone it's vodka. I pretend not to notice the person I'm talking to looking over my shoulder for the next conversation. I wonder if *they* notice I'm doing the same thing. If the host reads this, I'm sure I won't be on the mile-long guest list next year. Hopefully by next year, I really won't care.

In 1998, Meredith Brooks and I were nominated for a Grammy for Best Rock Song for "Bitch." There had been murmurings that this might happen, but I was distracted. I was pumping breast milk and going to Mommy & Me. I'll never forget it. The phone rang one morning at 7:00am, Meredith was out of breath—we got a nomination! I ran out to fetch the *L.A. Times* from the driveway. It's not that I didn't believe her; I just had to see it for myself. There it was—in black and beige.

I know people who have been nominated five times, won three times…statues on the mantles behind them in photos on their websites. I will never be one of them. That's okay. It wasn't our goal or even on our minds when we wrote that song. Thank you, Universe, for pouring me some gravy. How Fucking Fantastic.

The Grammys were being hosted in New York that year. Here are some things I remember:

- I treated myself to an overpriced silver sateen ensemble that I found at a boutique on the Sunset Strip. I could have just gone to Lohmann's, but I decided that for this occasion, I should shop somewhere a little more Rock Star. It's still hanging in my closet, though I haven't been able to button the pants for years.

- The night before the show, I was invited to a dinner for the nominees. We all had our picture taken with our medals around our necks. I asked for Adam to be next to me in mine. After all he was the one who "*wouldn't want it any other way.*" That framed portrait is the first thing I see when I walk into my office…in a more prominent position than any Gold or Platinum plaque.

- The winner of Best Rock Song was announced at the pre-telecast ceremony. Art Garfunkel was the host and he pronounced my name incorrectly. Can you imagine going through life with a name like Garfunkel and not taking more care in how you pronounce someone's name? It only hurt for a second. He went on to announce that The Wallflowers' "One Headlight" won the Grammy. At least we lost to a song I loved.

- I still felt like I won.

- Adam and I left five month old Layla with "Auntie" Jamie at her apartment on the Upper East Side. When we returned late that night Layla was sleeping in a stroller in the hallway with a note taped to her blanket saying, "I have diarrhea." Poor Layla. Poor Auntie Jamie.

After I returned to L.A. and started coming back down to earth, I was exiting a Starbucks one afternoon and who happened to hold the door open for me but Wallflower Jakob Dylan, writer of "One Headlight." You'd think I would have learned by now: just because the Universe gives you a chance to say something, doesn't mean you have to say it. But I sorta did:

"Hey Jakob…Your song beat out my song for a Grammy. But I really love 'One Headlight.' Well done."

He stared at me blankly. The poor guy was just trying to be a gentleman and hold the door, and I couldn't just say thank you. Of course I couldn't.

The Grammys will never be as exciting for me as they were that year.

Tonight I'll go to the party with Suzan and my bottle of water, and try to find my place in the crowd, where half the people won't know who the hell I am and the other half put me up so high on a pedestal that I'm afraid to fall. In my own mind, I'm somewhere in-between.

Grammy Party 2013. Me, Ian Kirkpatrick and Suzan. That very well might be Adam Lambert behind us on the right—with the drink—and the eyeliner.

The Future Always Comes

I'VE HAD A funny feeling lately. It's occurred to me...*I'm not in a rush.*
I've been multitasking since my daughter was born. Now it appears, I actually have some time on my hands again. I can't remember what I used to
do with it all.

When Layla was an infant, I wondered what it would be like when she
could hold her head up by herself. And when she could do that, I wondered
what it would be like when she could sit up; when she could walk...when
she could blow her nose on her own, tie a shoelace, cross the street (that one
was hard), beat an egg, light a candle (I'm *still* not comfortable with that). I
wasn't trying to fast forward. I simply *looked* forward...to the freedom the
next phase would bring.

Well, all these phases came. One after the other, like dominos. Soon,
our beautiful, clever, funny, smart daughter was spending the better part of
her time at home behind a closed bedroom door, bits and pieces of her day
revealed sparingly, if at all. When we handed her over the keys to a car, we
began seeing her less and less and we didn't have to drive her wherever it was
she wanted to go. I had wondered about *that* day too.

After all the years of staying put instead of venturing out, praying I
wouldn't forget a great idea because I couldn't document it fast enough,
child trumping *all,* I'm finally getting my independent groove back only
to find I'm secretly wishing Layla would pay more attention to me. Cuddle

up and watch a movie. Or put the phone down on our way to the mall…
in case something occurred to me that I'd like to share, although I wouldn't
want to spoil that pre-shopping euphoria by suggesting that simply being
in the moment with the person you are with should take precedence over
an electronic exchange with someone who isn't even in the car. What can I
say? We choose our battles. She's pulling away. I have to let her go. Another
domino. The future always comes. No way around it. It's closer than you
think.

Should I Stay or Should I Go

I WENT TO a session where a twenty-something topliner showed up. I was confused. I was supposed to be working with "Frannie," and I was looking forward to working with Frannie. I had heard great things about her, but this wasn't Frannie. The twenty-something replacement was dispatched by her handler because, I was told, Frannie "was sick." That's code for "a more desirable session came up for Frannie." Twenty-something was coming off of a huge hit, but had not written anything else of significance.

When we were introduced she said, "Oh…I've heard of you. You were 'all that' in the '90s."

At first I thought, *Why, thank you.* And then I realized it wasn't a compliment. (It reminded me of something young Juliette said to middle-aged Rayna in the pilot of "Nashville"—that her mama used to listen to Rayna's music when she [Juliettte] was still in her belly.)

When I started out in this business, I was twenty-four. Everyone else was around that age too, and we had much in common. Now, I'm older than some of the mothers who drop their kids off to write with me. I took my age off my Wiki page, but whom am I fooling? When my song, "Had Me at Hello" won a Radio Disney Award for Best Crush Song, I was in the audience having a hot flash.

I'm sure you won't be surprised to know I've been doing a lot of thinking about how much longer I want to stay in the game. When asked the question, I usually reply, "As long as I'm still having fun." Lately I've been asking myself if I am—having fun that is. They say if you have to ask yourself if you're hungry, you're probably not. Uh oh.

Maybe I'm supposed to stop now and start enjoying the fruits of my labor. But what if I want just one more apple? Or even a tiny little grape? I might just have to open my mind to the possibility that my modest handful of hits *was* my fifteen minutes. What a humbling and sobering possibility, but a possibility nonetheless.

Not long after the Frannie session I was on yet another songwriting speed date with three more hopeful hit-makers; we had some semblance of a hook but no title. In the context of the storyline, the title needed to be a word or group of words that had something to do with sticking together. It also would be advantageous if it rhymed with "let go" since those two words were at the end of an upcoming line. I thought of something I didn't actually take seriously but in the spirit of Daring To Suck I blurted it out.

"How about 'Legos'…we stick together like Legos."

In my mind it was a placeholder for a better idea. But then, everyone's eyes bugged and before I knew it that was our title. My instincts told me it was far too juvenile, even for a child star on *Nickelodeon*. Then again, they're getting younger and younger. Maybe a fetus could record it.

Seriously, Legos? I couldn't have been less interested in what I was doing. My mind kept wandering to how many carbs there were in the protein bar at the bottom of my purse.

Before we had a chance to sleep on it, and perhaps re-assess the song *ourselves*, one of the hopeful hit-makers consulted his publisher. The publisher's opinion was that Legos wouldn't cut it. I wasn't surprised. I knew how ridiculous it was. But that wasn't the reason he thought it wouldn't work: Apparently, Ed Sheeran, had beaten us to it. He had just released a song called "Lego House." Who knew? I swear I didn't. And I don't think anyone else did either, because if they did, they should have *said* something.

So here's what went through my mind…

- I was *kidding* about that title. I had no idea that everyone would react favorably. So I must be *Out of Touch*.

- But…the hopeful hit-makers loved it…so maybe I *am IN Touch*.

- But…it's already part of the name of a current hit song…*Out of Touch*

- But…apparently I am channeling words that are trending in hit song titles…*SO in Touch*.

- But…if I'd been doing my homework, I would have known that song existed and not gone there…*Out of Touch*.

- I'm going backwards. I'm writing inconsequential songs again. At least I know it. *IN Touch!*

Why do I continue to put myself in this position? Running around haphazardly swapping partners in search of—the same song. Am I writing what I love or am I chasing a formula based on algorithms and listening behavior? I knew the answer.

Once again, I pondered the definition of crazy.

Like Andy said to Red in *The Shawshank Redemption:* "Get busy living or get busy dying." It was clear I was at a crossroads and I needed to find another way to make my work matter to *me*.

P.S. Legos was replaced by Velcro: a contribution made by the hopeful hit-maker's publisher. I hope that someday he gets to enjoy his piece of pie.

Snapshot: Complicated

I'm driving the kids to school, happily listening to the news on NPR. Layla connects her iPod to a cable in my glove compartment and a catchy guitar abruptly replaces *Morning Edition.* The latest song they can't get enough of? "Complicated,"— Avril Lavigne. It was a huge hit when they were five. I think to myself, *that's* interesting.

"Have you heard her *new* single?" I ask. They don't care about her new single. They want "Complicated." I wonder why. Maybe it's because it has a specific point of view. It's void of sonic trickery, yet it still sounds fresh and edgy. They sing it word-for-word at the top of their fifteen-year-old lungs. I am thoroughly entertained. The news can wait.

Carpool.

Tick Tock

ON THE FIRST day Layla drove herself to school, I ran out of the house in my robe and slippers and signaled for her to open the passenger window. There was a very important message I needed to bestow. I held my hand to my heart and gushed about how divine it was going to be for her—driving around with *no one else in the car!* How certain thoughts would only occur when there was *no one else in the car!* How sacred and uncharted new territory was about to unfold. How whatever it is you are listening to (whether it's the rage of "Helter Skelter" or the zen of Bon Iver) connects in some perfect or perfectly incongruous way to whatever it is in the frame of your windshield.

I don't think I actually said all of this, but I thought it and managed to cram most of it into a few urgent sentences.

She humored me, *"Yes Mama…Okay Mama."*

She let me go on but I could tell she couldn't wait to put her foot on the accelerator and be free…like the first gasp of a new life. Another rite of passage. She checked her mirrors and fastened her seatbelt.

When she was finally out of view, I stood on the curb clutching my robe in the haze and confusion of all the letting go and wondered if the first song she heard while driving away would take her back to that morning for the rest of her life…if she will ever experience the nostalgia I have become so fond of myself…if her generation will look back and have the same meaningful connection to songs. Most hits rise and fall more quickly than ever, enter and exit our consciousness so much faster. How can any song have a realistic chance of putting a solid notch in a young girl's (or boy's) time-line in this here-today gone-*today* world? With all the devices, hyperactive camera work, pop up ads, real *and* virtual multi-tasking, it's hard to stay focused on one thing. No wonder there's a surge of ADD.

Will Layla turn on the radio (or its equivalent) in twenty years and feel her heart skip a beat from a song that transports her back to an unforgettable kiss? Only time will tell.

Bon Voyage, my little chick. Text me when you get there.

The Pitch

I GREW UP with a boy named Mike. When Mike grew up he had a daughter named Jen. When Jen grew up she wanted to work in the Hollywood film and TV industry. She came to L.A. full of light and ideas. She worked for a few companies as an assistant and then as a junior manager at an established talent agency. I've seen her name listed as producer on a couple of movie posters. Her career is coming along quite nicely.

When Mike and his wife Doris come to L.A. to visit Jen, occasionally we gather at my house. Jen gets a kick out of hearing tales from the frontline of the songwriting world. One Thanksgiving, she suggested that these tales might make a great TV series. Little Jen. I changed her diaper once.

To me, what I did every day wasn't so novel, especially, in *this* town. To Jen, whose job it was to have her ear to the ground, I offered an insider's perspective that was amusing. She was very persuasive and I loved her enthusiasm, but I didn't know the first thing about writing a pilot. I told her if she found someone who did, I would make myself available and be there to tell my stories.

Not surprisingly, Jen found "Jann," who had talent and some success behind her. Jen and Jann asked me to compile as many vignettes about my experiences as possible, to give Jann plenty of windows into the world of the changing music business.

I remembered the journal entries I had written when I was pregnant. The ones in a folder buried in the recesses of my computer's hard drive. I dug them up. I had even more tales to tell now. So I wrote, and I wrote and I wrote. And I found myself coming to life. Like a flower being sprinkled by rain. It was different than writing songs. I wasn't putting words in anyone's mouth. I didn't have to rhyme. I didn't have to second-guess myself because what I was telling was the truth. I wasn't competing or trying to impress anyone. I found it just as satisfying writing about my many disappointments as my handful of successes. Maybe Jen was on to something. I was eager to see how Jann would incorporate my narratives.

The series I fantasized was along the lines of a "Sex in the City," where the protagonist would come home after a day in the life and think, wonder and perhaps blog about the business and how it was changing, and the effect it had on her, other writers, artists, fans, wallets, ethics…etc. It would be humorous, cynical, humiliating, exhilarating, and absurd, the gamut of emotions a serial songwriter typically faces on a given day.

As it turned out, the pilot Jann came up with was full of characters that were unfamiliar to me. It was a dramedy about a songwriter who got out of the business to raise a family and needed to get back in because of her husband's financial blunders. The plot had no resemblance to my life. Clearly, we had different ideas about the show we wanted to create, but Jen and Jann were in agreement that we'd have a better shot at getting one off the ground with Jann's pilot than with the one I envisioned. I was a novice. They weren't. So I went along. If we were successful, it would give us an opportunity to get our feet wet, and give *me* an opportunity down the line to tell another story. Mine.

Hollywood heavyweight, Gale Anne Hurd, signed on as our producer. *That* was a better start than we could have hoped for. We had Lionsgate and MGM interested for an L.A. minute, until one "creative" who was into our pitch was replaced; another decided he wanted something more youth driven and another wanted something more mature. Still another liked it, but what she was *really* looking for was a plot that involved aliens. Sometimes it seemed like nobody knew *what* they wanted. Our pitching process ran its course and we put the pilot on the back burner. I wasn't as disappointed as I thought I'd be, because I had found so much joy in all that writing.

THAT CHRISTMAS I received an email from my friend and colleague, Billy ("Like a Virgin") Steinberg. He sends one out every year to a number of his friends, and poses a music-related question such as, "What are your ten favorite bands of all time?" or "What are your five favorite songs they recorded?" You can answer the question simply or you can go into detail. Billy then consolidates and shares the results.

Or you could ignore it, like I always had. This time, for whatever reason, I decided to jump in. I wrote about those classics and how they beam me back…and I'm young again and I'm at that party with *that* boy.

I love writing about this stuff. I could do it every day.

A few days later, Billy told me that his sister-in-law had mentioned how entertained she was by my comments. Right then I felt a tiny little fire start—small as the flame on a matchstick. Sometimes that's all it takes.

The very next morning, as I slipped my feet into my slippers, I looked over at Adam and told him I wanted to write a book. Because, while I was writing about what I loved and what I *knew*, I was transformed—happy again. Like a fish back in water, smiling, as I tapped away at the keyboard, Carrie Bradshaw-style; it felt real and raw and right. I liked it. Wherever it was going—and it surely felt like it was going someplace.

Truth is, I missed having a dream. It had been so long since I allowed myself the pleasure. Maybe I was afraid because dreams don't always come true. No excuse. That's the fastest way to grow old. Stop dreaming.

I called Jesse in N.Y., remembering that after he placed my first piece in *She*, he had encouraged me to continue writing especially if the stories involved my body of work; something I didn't have at that time. Now I did. We had fallen a bit out of touch over the years. He was married and busy raising two beautiful daughters of his own, but he was still there, and our bond was no less strong. Jesse got me. He always got me. I said, "I'm ready now." "Wanna read some stories?"

With Jesse Nash at Uncle Lulu's, circa 1983.

A Little Help from My Friends

I RECEIVED AN email from the aforementioned Chris Mann after "The Voice—Season 2." At least ten thousand other people did too. As a savvy contestant he had learned how to get his social media on. He didn't win, but he came close. And he was determined to milk it for all it was worth.

The email informed me that "Chris is going to be on 'Ellen' tomorrow." He asks that I set my DVR, and suggests that after the show I head over to his Facebook page (head over? how far away is it? do I need to get gas?) or Tweet him to let him know how he did on "Ellen" (in case he wasn't sure himself). Also, I should be sure to use the hash tag #ChrisMannEllen so he can find the correct Tweets. And…can we send a Tweet to @TheEllenShow or visit "The Ellen Show" on Facebook (do I need to bring a gift?) and thank her for having him on. Wow…that's a lot of stuff for me to do.

Wait, there was more. Just in case I missed it, Chris announced air dates for his PBS special, "Chris Mann in Concert: A Mann for All Seasons" and his first headlining tour! Visit his website for details Chrismannmusic.com or follow him on Facebook, Twitter, YouTube and Instagram. I am dizzy!

You can't blame him. He is doing what he has to do. It's the new paradigm. He has no choice but to solicit support unabashedly, if he doesn't want to get lost in the crowd. And it *is* crowded out there. It seems like there are more people vying for attention than ever before. Suzan puts things in perspective: "Artists used to have fan clubs. Other people ran them. Now, an artist is the head of his/her own fan club." It can't be that difficult, because everyone tweets…your local pharmacy…plastic surgeons…the Pope.

I thought I'd try to get a little social networking going myself, so I asked Layla to set me up with a Facebook profile. It would actually serve two purposes: I'd get to see what all the fuss was about *and* I could monitor *her* profile to make sure she wasn't posting anything inappropriate for all the world to see. Turns out *she* was the one who insisted *I* remove pictures of *me*. Anything with cleavage or a cocktail in my hand had to go. What a party pooper. She showed me how to make "friends," tag friends, post on my timeline, click on links and see my activity (in case *I* forgot what *I* was doing).

I saw what childhood playmates looked like. I thought, "Who *are* all these old people?" I scrolled my News Feed and caught up on vacations, marriages, births, deaths, record deals, first singles, concertgoers, current president-lovers, current president-haters, baseball fans, haircuts, pet tricks…and a whole lot of "humblebrags" (passive-aggressive self-promotion).

I searched for and re-connected with my college roommate, Kathy, who deserted me for a boyfriend during our junior year in college. She apologized retroactively, eloquently and sincerely for the pain she had caused. She said she had wanted to find me and tell me how she felt for years. I had been devastated when I lost her and it felt good to remember how much I loved her and to know she loved me too.

And, I confess, I accepted a bunch of friendship requests under false pretenses. I wasn't really that interested in the friendships. I would never have agreed to meet those people for coffee.[1] I accepted because I posted a video and wanted them to "like" it. But, because I accepted all those requests, I started getting inundated with invitations to "like" things from strangers who now called me their friend. They weren't interested in *my* friendship. They'd never have agreed to meet *me* for coffee.

I was getting so bombarded with all those annoying little Facebook beeps that I started "un-friending" people. It was very unfriendly of me,

---

[1] This was Suzan's barometer as to whether or not you should accept someone's "friendship." She has since expanded her criteria.

but I couldn't take it any more. I don't want to be invited to "like" anything that I wasn't drawn to on my own. Gone are the days when you heard about something just because it was that good. I think it was called "word of mouth."

Shortly after I started working on this book, I had a conversation with Sarah, the literary agent of a real live human friend of mine. My real live human friend had sent her some of my material and she was kind enough to give a constructive critique. I was prepared for her to tell me to stick to writing songs. On the contrary, she was encouraging. And she said this:

"You definitely have a voice. If you want your story to take on a life of its own, you're going to have to brand yourself…make sure people know who you are. Get some more stories published, make sure you have visibility on a Facebook fan page, consider a blog, set up a website…any five-year-old can help you with this. And also, you might want to get a Twitter account."

I think I'll call Chris for some guidance.

To my friend Chris Mann: consider all of this unsolicited complimentary publicity from one real live human friend to another.

Accidentally on Purpose

ALL THIS VENTING has been so cathartic. I'm not sure what else there is to say. Jesse suggests it would be advantageous if I had one more vignette about a well-known recording artist. Celebrities feed the beast. I'm sorry, Jesse. I don't. He asks if I'm absolutely *sure* I didn't get a shot with Britney when I was in the studio with her. Yes, I'm sure. Don't remind me. I guess I could find a picture of her next to someone, (preferably a dancer with a rock-hard body) and cut and paste my head over theirs like I did in the photo with Chrissie Hynde.

Actually, there *was* another noteworthy artist I worked with that I haven't written about (and with whom I have no photo), because nothing remarkable (and that's not a diss) transpired. Producer (no " " necessary) John Shanks asked me to come to the studio to write with him and a rising star from Nashville…I mean Australia…I mean Nashville…okay—both. Keith Urban.

Keith was unassuming. He seemed *just like one of us*, and he sort of *was* at the time. His face wasn't on the cover of *People*…yet. John and Keith strapped on guitars; *SongSex* was had. Keith came to my house a couple of days later to write another song. To be honest? It wasn't the same without John and I have nothing to show for that second session except a work tape. (Someone once asked me if I'd ever considered putting it on eBay. No, I haven't, and I never would).

The song we wrote with John, "Whenever I Run," was included on Keith's first album, *Golden Road*. I didn't see Keith until ten years later when I went to a Stones concert at the Staples Center. There he was shredding on "It's Only Rock 'n Roll (But I Like It)." My how far we've come. Not *just like one of us* anymore.

Soon after that concert, our paths crossed again in a more ordinary environment. I belong to a small tennis club. It's not fancy like L.A.'s Brentwood or Riviera and it's a fraction of the cost to become a member. I heard through the grapevine that Keith and Nicole (Kidman) joined. *That* was interesting. Why? Didn't they have their own private pool and tennis court? And if not, why did they choose to join *this* very unassuming establishment?

So, one day I was watching Layla play tennis and out of the corner of my eye I saw a figure floating toward me—a statuesque, porcelain-skinned, flaming-haired, larger-than-life celestial being. She was looking straight ahead, so as not to make eye contact with anyone. I didn't realize it was Nicole until she had passed. Following close behind in a baseball cap was scruffy-haired Keith. I wanted to shout, "Hey Keith!" However, my fear was, "What if he doesn't remember me?" *That* would be embarrassing. Maybe I don't give myself enough credit. But before I could make up my mind, he and Nicole were rallying on court five.

Now, in general, it's not cool to *approach* (here we go again) celebrities at our tennis club. Much less ask for that photo you never took for a book you may be writing. How very star-stalker that would be. This is a place where a person of fame can count on having his or her privacy respected. Then there's Adam. He was the board president at the time. He would not have been pleased.

The truth is it would've been nice to say, "Hi" to Keith for reasons other than getting a photo. It's not like I had *no* history with the man. We *had SongSex*, after all. If he *hadn't* become so famous, I *would* have said "Hey" in a heartbeat. So, what I was doing (or *not* doing) was the opposite of star-stalking, wasn't it? It was purposeful "star-privacy-respecting." If he chose to join *this* particular no-frills tennis club, wasn't it possible he *wanted* the experience of being a mere mortal to balance out nights when he was on stage with Mick? Perhaps it was his choice to stay in touch with how it feels to be *just like one of us.* I don't know. I'm projecting. Again. It's also possible that Nicole was preparing for a movie role in which she plays a tennis pro, but I *want* to believe the former.

So, I've decided if I see Keith Urban in the near future reading by the pool or pushing his kid on a swing, I'm going to say "Hey." And I might ask him if he minds taking a little photo with me to be included in my potential memoir—half rock star, half one of us. If he says, "Hey" back and he doesn't mind taking a selfie? Great. If not, I can always use this:

Insert Shelly Here!

To Sell or Not to Sell

THE DESK IN my office was a mess. I hadn't been going in there for a while. In fact, my computer had been planted on the counter in my kitchen—the heart of my home, where I felt very centered. There were a dozen Post-it notes surrounding it. The counter is for cooking, not working, but there was something about my office I was avoiding.

I signed my first song publishing deal in 1991, back when publishing companies signed writers simply because they believed in them and were willing to take a chance. There didn't have to be anything substantial in their royalty pipeline. That was a long time ago. My contract with Hit & Run Music stipulated that they would own and control my songs "forever" in exchange for a reasonable advance. I never had a regret. That advance was enough to buy me freedom, have some choices and drive that sweet car.

When the agreement was renegotiated in 1994, my meticulously conscientious attorney, Mark, implemented a provision that would have the ownership of my songs revert back to me in 2013. That year was so far away, I put it out of my mind. But like I said: the future always comes. And it came again. Thank you Mark.

Mark and I had an ongoing discussion about how I would manage my "catalog" of songs when they reverted; a catalog that includes my handful of hits ("Bitch," "What a Girl Wants," "Come on over Baby," "Almost Doesn't Count," "I Wanna Be with You") and many other lesser known, but royalty-generating titles. Some writers arrange for their royalties to be collected on their behalf by a company of their choice for a small administration fee. Others choose to sell their catalog for a *big fat payday*. It's a serious decision; for once you sell, you say goodbye. You forgo authority and control.

I've always felt there was something enviable about being in a position that would allow you to "sell your catalog." I've heard colleagues I admire talk about selling *theirs*. It made them seem so accomplished. If I was at the point where *I* could sell mine, didn't it mean that *I* had reached this upper echelon, joined the ranks of the elite? (And, that I was lucky enough to have had a savvy lawyer who insisted on that reversion clause many years ago.)

It wasn't long before potential buyers caught wind of my catalog becoming available and an offer came in to purchase it for a more-than-fair price. It seemed like a no-brainer. There were tax incentives and I'd have a nice sum I could invest and watch grow. It wasn't without hesitation, but I said okay, and we were off and running. Emails were flying. Piles of statements were copied and delivered. Contracts were drawn up.

Then a funny thing happened. I started waking up in the middle of the night with a pain in my heart. Something didn't feel right. I was the bride at the altar who knew she shouldn't get married. (And, I knew how that felt because I'd been there.) I was the birth mother who decides in the eleventh hour she can't give up the baby.

I lay awake thinking I was abandoning my songs. I realized I was more connected to them than I thought. How could I send them away so easily after they just returned home? Maybe that's why I was working in my kitchen. I couldn't look my office in the eye.

I called Mark and told him I was having second thoughts. He had never encouraged me to sell in the first place, but he *had* supported my decision. Calm and level-headed, he reminded me of all the reasons *I* wanted to make this move…the bird in hand…the financial security…the uncertain state of the music business…it *was* probably a good time to cash out. I got off the phone and felt somewhat relieved. The relief was temporary though—like when you have the stomach flu and you know you're going to be sick—and after you puke you feel better, but ten minutes later…

I went about the next few days in denial, telling myself that I was a wimp, that other people do it all the time. So I called some of those other people, and asked them if they were sorry that they sold. Billy said *yes*. Annie said *no*. Kevin said *yes*. Beth said *no*—a lot of help they were.

Industry experts will warn you to be realistic about the future earning power of your songs. Apparently, many successful songwriters have a fantasy that a huge placement in a Steven Spielberg film or a Coke commercial in the Super Bowl will come along, so they don't sell, only to regret it years later, when Steven and Coca-Cola never call, and they've missed their opportunity for that *big payday*. You're better off taking the cash.

But won't I be betting against myself if I sell? How can I expect the Universe to give my songs love, if I deny them my own? It's always been possibility, *not guarantee that compels me. Besides, this isn't the stock market or the horse races. I'm not at a casino. These aren't poker chips. This is my life. My songs are an extension of me. How can I put a dollar value on them?*

I kept waking up with that stupid pain in my heart. You can do all the math you want. You can be shown PowerPoint presentations that illustrate to every last detail why something is prudent. But even though it may make perfect sense, it doesn't explain why you can't sleep and all the Ambien in the world doesn't help.

I called Mark and told him I was having *third* thoughts. He's known me for a long time. He wasn't surprised. Mark said the songs were talking to me. I love him for that. He said he'd call the buyer. I said I'd woman up and make the call myself.

So...did I move out of my office because it was too painful to sit amidst the Platinum records and not hear the phone ring as much as it used to? *Yes.* Did I move out because the music business I fell in love with doesn't exist anymore? *Yes.* And did I move out because I don't want to face the fact that a chapter in my life is drawing to a close and the thought of moving on to a new chapter is scary? *Yes, yes, yes* and *yes.* But my decision was made.

I'm not selling my songs. Nobody is going to care as much about them, no matter what they say or intend to do.

I woke up the next morning and realized I slept like a baby. I didn't even get up to pee. I carried my computer back into my office, straightened my desk and dusted off my lava lamp, and, I made that call.

So You Want to Be a Songwriter

I DON'T BLAME you. And if that's the case, here are some words of advice:

- **Practically Speaking…**In the modern songwriting business, it behooves an aspiring songwriter to circulate (*network, network, network)*. No matter how effective a publisher can be, remember, it's competitive for them too. Once, they were able to recoup a songwriter's advance from album sales. Since that's no longer possible, there are less publishing deals being made. And there are more of *you* than ever before. Get out. Go to showcases, recording studios, industry hangs. Talk to *everyone*. This business is about relationships. You never know what's going to happen or where it's going to come from. *Nothing* will happen if you stay home. Consider a manager. Managers are taking over much of what traditional publishers used to do: pitch songs and get you in the right room. Bottom line: like Suzan said, you're the head of your own fan club. Don't expect anyone to do it for you. Sell yourself.

- **Stay Tuned…**to the latest hits. This is more important if you're an aspiring songwriter than an aspiring artist. New artists can break ground with a fresh sound. But in general (and this doesn't mean there aren't exceptions), mainstream radio cleaves to the familiar. If you're looking for representation, or you're hoping to get invited to a camp, playing them an original song that sounds like it's already *on* the radio is a pretty good ticket in. Once you do that, then go out and have fun breaking all the rules.

- **Supplement...** In the current state of the ecosystem, it goes without saying (at least until further notice), one may not be able to count on songwriting royalties alone to pay the bills. Perhaps there's something else within the spectrum of the music business that you'd be good at and would earn you income, while keeping your sense of purpose. Consider parallel fields: engineering, mixing, booking, arranging, or teaching. You may even choose to look outside the boundaries of the industry: drive an Uber, moonlight as a bartender, put your graphic skills to use. It's quite possible you might meet someone in that car or at that bar who will play an instrumental role in your success.

- **Believing in Yourself Trumps All...** Forget all the warnings. Forget anything anyone told you about how hard it is to make it in the music business (including me). When you really want to do something, all the warnings in the world won't matter. You might hear them but they won't resonate. You'll proceed with blinders on. If a song is sub par you'll write another. Somewhere inside you, you have to believe you are the exception. You *must* think that way. Despite all the obstacles, the Universe tends to shine more light on those who believe in something hard enough. I know it's true. I've seen it with my own eyes.

Little Earthquakes

CHANGING THE WORLD was never my intention. What I always wanted to do was shift the Universe in some small way. We're all mere mortals. Maybe it's my own hubris talking, but if I write a song that connects with someone…makes their day a little better…I will feel like I made a difference. Which doesn't exactly make me any less mortal, but sometimes it makes me *feel* like I am. Perhaps it's not a footprint on the moon, but it's something. Energy is infinite.

A few years ago, I received a letter in the mail from someone who went to an L.A. Circle Showcase where I performed. The writer told me that when she was in junior high school her best friend's parents allowed their daughter (and friends) to write anything they wanted on her bedroom wall. Her contribution was the lyrics to my song. She said that "Bitch" was every girl's anthem and it made her proud to be a woman, even at the tender age of 13.

Really? "Every girl's anthem?" Thank you. I mean, really, thank you for telling me that. That made me feel *so good*.

Then there was this: Six thousand miles away in London, Ruth Anderson-Davis has been sitting behind a computer in an office at the major publishing giant that bought little Hit & Run, sending me Excel reports to help me keep track of film and TV license requests. After much professional correspondence, she got a little personal:

She thought I might enjoy hearing about it? I don't think she could have given me a sweeter gift. Something unusual and positive happened out there because of *my* song. This business is crowded. Every song is merely one on an infinite playlist that is just getting longer. Mine, at least for that moment, had mattered. It was generous of Ruth to let me know. I printed her email and taped it on the wall next to my desk, so I wouldn't forget.

Ruth Anderson-Davis ✐   8:28 AM   RA
To: Shelly Peiken   APPROVAL CONFUSION ▢
RE: Your Quarterly Synch report

I'd just like to share something with you Shelly if I may – I was in a clothes store last Saturday and "Bitch" came on over the in store music system... when the chorus kicked in, (no word of a lie) every woman in there started singing along (about 15 of us) and when we realised we were all doing it we laughed and raised our voices and sang the whole chorus together loudly! All random strangers. It was like something from a film that never really happens in real life – spontaneous, unifying and empowering – I wish you could have seen it. Made me smile and thought you might enjoy hearing about it.

Have a great weekend.

Ruth

Ruth Anderson-Davis| Music Publishing | +44

I didn't speak to dear Ruth for a while after that, but I would email her from time to time with a few questions that I knew only she could answer. Of course, she would reply immediately, saying she would try her best to be of assistance. Then one day she told me that sadly, she was being "made redundant" (that's British for being let go.)

I asked Ruth for her phone number because I was coming to London the following month and I wanted to take her to dinner. I needed to tell her in person that just as I had shifted her Universe with my song, she had shifted mine with her message.

Plus, I wanted to thank her. Not just because of the all the spreadsheets, or the thoughtful email, but because she made me realize *I* need to make sure *I* tell people when they enrich *my* life, and not assume that they know.

Because, they might not...and if they are anything like me, at some point when they've lost their way, or they've been made redundant, or they are not sure how much they matter, it will mean everything.

Ruth and me dining at The Ampersand Hotel in London.

Landsliding

WHEN I WAS young, there was a boy I couldn't seem to stop loving. I had loved him for so long I couldn't imagine waking up one day and not having that to do. That unrequited love was part of my identity. How scary to let that go. Now, it is my family I've built my life around, and I've loved *them* for even longer.

Time has made me bolder. Change, as much as we try to deny it and avoid it, energizes and surprises. We have a choice: We can fight it every step of the way or we can sail through the changing tides of the ocean with an open heart.

The Gap

I LOVE MY life and what I do. I wake up every day and write a song. It's like having a meal or taking a shower, or drinking water. But some time during the summer of 2013 it hit me: Is there still room for me? If there is, do I even want to be here? If I don't want to be here, where should I go?

Now that I have grown up to be someone, can I become someone else?

Every time I heard Coldplay singing, *"I'm in the gap between the two trapezes,"* from their song "Every Teardrop Is a Waterfall," Layla squeezed my hand so I wouldn't cry. That made me cry more.

It's too late for a mid-life crisis. Maybe I should have had one and gotten it over with.

For the first time in my life, I was considering asking my doctor for a prescription for Zoloft.

I spoke to friends who were compassionate and loving. Some tried to encourage me by telling me my ennui would pass, or that the pendulum would swing. Others said, maybe it was time to get out of the music business...all honest heartfelt responses. They made me feel a little better simply by listening.

Many years ago, before anybody knew my name, I was fixed up to write with Allee ("Boogie Wonderland") Willis. Allee was the poster child for unconventional—famous for thinking outside the box. With her asymmetric shaggy hair and colorful baggy suits, she was the self-proclaimed Queen of Kitsch. Outside her bright pink house were bowling balls and gravel beds. Inside were collections of odd dolls, lunch boxes, Elvis statues, avant-garde art, vintage salt-and-pepper shakers and Grammys for huge hit records. Unfortunately, the songs *we* wrote together were forgettable (she wouldn't disagree). It wasn't until decades later that I would see why Allee was part of my journey.

Over the years I'd spot Allee across the room at an awards dinner—same asymmetric hair and baggy suit. You couldn't miss her. More recently I saw her at a mutual friend's birthday party. I was fairly sure she had no recollection of who I was, so I decided to find out. Not only did she remember me, she remembered the names of our forgettable songs. She asked if I wanted to have coffee or dinner some time. I took it as sign that the Universe wanted us to reconnect.

I was in the middle of my ongoing funk the day we were to convene. I didn't think I'd be good company, but I didn't want to disappoint the Universe. So I went. I knew I couldn't fake being cheerful, so I told Allee what I was going through, about being in The Gap. And without hesitation, Allee said:

"*The Gap*? That's the best place to be. You are the most fertile when you don't know where the hell you are, or where you're going. Anything can happen." She seemed quite certain. Defiant even. What an encouraging perspective…one that wasn't an option from a multiple-choice list of things to say to a heavy-hearted pal.

Allee recommended I read a book called *The Places That Scare You*. She said the author, Pema Chödrön, suggests *we try to get comfortable in that place of least comfort…If we're having a hard time don't try to push it away… have no expectation.* It sounded like Pema Chödrön was talking about The Gap! I had walked into the restaurant that evening cheerless and dejected, but I left skipping to my car.

A few weeks later, I went to Allee's one-night-only, one-woman show, which was to encompass all aspects of her life story: her childhood, growing up in Detroit, her work, her play, her hits, her hair. The stage was full of colorful kitschy props: plastic palm trees, rubber furniture, party favors. A few production assistants buzzed about. Front and center was a projector, a large screen (which I imagined was for displaying song lyrics, photos and videos) and a podium for Allee to lead the way. Downstage left was her tech guy with a laptop who would trigger audio-visuals upon Allee's cues.

When the show started, everything that could have gone wrong, did. First, a video wouldn't load properly. Then, when Allee signaled for a song lyric to be projected, her personal iPhoto album popped up instead. She and tech guy held up a poster board to block the screen, which then started wobbling on the verge of collapse. It was a complete technological fiasco. Nothing went as planned in front of an audience of hundreds of Hollywood heavies. If that had been me, I would have passed out on the podium. But Allee talked her way through it. It certainly wasn't visually dazzling and I can't say that the audience wasn't feeling uneasy, but the show went on.

The very next day I had a meeting with Jay Landers at Universal Records. I go back with Jay. In 1992, he asked Albert Hammond (Sr.) if he would write with me and Albert said, "Yes." I was grateful.

Jay asked me if I'd be interested in writing a song for Barbra Streisand. "It should be Donna Summer, 'She Works Hard for the Money,' meets Beyoncé, 'Crazy in Love.'" He envisioned a duet between Barbra and Beyoncé. (I knew Jay had a longstanding relationship with Barbra. I wasn't sure how he was going to swing Beyoncé.) Regardless, as much as I would have loved to try to write that song, I didn't think I was the girl for the job. (Besides, I knew what a long shot it was, if there was even a shot at all.) Jay needed someone far more outside the box than I venture. Someone who can fly by the seat of her...*baggy pants*. I knew who that was, of course: Allee Willis. Jay agreed. I was off the hook. Then, Jay asked if I would write it *with* her.

The next week I was back at Allee's after twenty years. Same bowling balls. Same pink house, fish bowls filled with M&Ms and jellybeans. I couldn't help but wonder if maybe *this* was the something that was going to happen in The Gap. We were going to write a *big fat hit* for Barbra and Beyoncé. *That* would be worth me having lost my compass for a while.

I asked Allee if she had recovered from the train wreck of that show. (I didn't use those exact words.) I thought she was going to say she was refunding every ticket buyer's money. Instead, she said, "Are you kidding? I'm working on my *next* show." The glass doesn't get more half full than that.

We attempted to write an EDM (electronic dance music) song *without* a backing track to fluff us. It was called, "Misunderestimated." (That's not a word, but it *should* be a word.) We snapped our fingers and sang *a capella* into our iPhones, and with a couple of taps and swipes forwarded it to Jay to show Barbra.

He loved it. Naturally, there were a few tweaks, and then a few more tweaks. A few more voice memos—and then—there was no word for about four months. Although Jay *had* warned us it could take a while, we *knew* no news for that long was not good news. Finally, I received an email fom him explaining that the project had changed direction and Barbra was leaning towards an all-*male* duet album..."therefore your song with AW doesn't fit." AW? Is she a *root beer* now? He expressed his appreciation and I know he was sincere. (I still love that song title, and I hope to use it again someday.)

Meanwhile, I got a hold of Pema Chödrön's book that Allee recommended. The passage that spoke to me the loudest was: "*We can try to control the uncontrollable by looking for security and predictability, always hoping to be comfortable and safe. But the truth is we can never avoid uncertainty. This not knowing is part of the adventure, and it's also what makes us afraid.*"

I'd like to say I've had a great epiphany, taken a quantum leap. I'd like to say a sign appeared with fireworks and fanfare to let me know a seismic change was about to take place. It's been *nothing* like that.

Here's what *did* happen: I got comfortable in The Gap. Now I wake up every morning and practice being brave. By no means am I giving up writing songs. I've just stopped working with collaborators whose processes and attitudes are not harmonious with mine. If I have writer's block, I make soup. I know I'm in a good place because I haven't the need for as much retail therapy. If I'm anxious and can't sleep, I remind myself it's *always* better in the morning.

The Universe is conspiring with me to make something happen, as it has been all along. I just don't know what it is yet. I'm in The Gap. I'm not supposed to know.

What I *do* know is that when I picked up where I left off writing these stories, I started walking with a spring in my step. It's like I have a little secret. I don't want the Zoloft anymore. I'm right where I'm supposed to be—in pursuit—feeling hopeful. And, very fertile.

Allee Willis.

I Hope You Dance

WHEN LAYLA WAS almost three years old, Lee Ann Womack released a song called "I Hope You Dance." The lyric was an eloquent and heart-warming list of hopes we have for our children inspired by the lessons we've learned ourselves. And yes, it was a *country* smash.

> *I hope you still feel small when you stand beside the ocean.*
> *Whenever one door closes I hope one more opens.*
> *Promise me that you'll give faith a fighting chance.*
> *And when you get the choice to sit it out or dance,*
> *I Hope You Dance.*

I'm not sure this song would have had its way with me if I didn't have a child, but I do. So many times I see my daughter on the verge of making a decision...standing on the edge...toe in the water...thinking, "should I or shouldn't I?" And because of that song, I hear a voice in my head, and I catch myself whispering, "Dance, Layla, dance!"

Take the chances I didn't. Be not as fearful or prideful as I know I have been in my life. God knows, I haven't danced enough. I've stood in the corner watching, envious of the ones spinning under the lights. I've been a spectator on the sidelines wishing I were on the field bracing for the ball. I've been afraid to sing at the top of my lungs for fear my voice would crack.

I know there are times I have been brave, but I have enough regrets to wish I'd have been braver.

So thank you Tia Sillers and Mark D. Sanders, co-writers of "I Hope You Dance," for doing something I strive to do every day, but only succeed in occasionally. Thank you for writing a song that makes a girl pull over to the side of the road to catch her breath; a song that makes her want to never write another song again, if it can't be *that* song. A song that speaks to the part of her heart where all her dreams and wishes for her child are stored.

And, a song that has *that* message—a universal sentiment in a unique frame: It isn't *insisting* you dance. It's suggesting you do. And that was brilliant. For, as any parent knows, the best way to get your child *not* to do something is to tell them to do it. The most you can do is hope they will.

Dance Layla, dance.

Afterword

THE HEATED DEBATE over the distribution of income from streaming music was surging right around the time I was crossing the t's and dotting the i's of this book and continues to this day. The digital revolution has dramatically changed the way we listen to music, but the laws that govern the way songwriters are paid for their content have still not caught up with technology.

In addition, online piracy is alive and thriving. Tech companies have fought against efforts to curb unauthorized file sharing because of the tremendous revenue they earn selling advertising beside it.

These companies also have a financial interest in keeping streaming rates low and have been successful in maintaining the status quo—in fact they are making efforts to *lower* the status quo. But there are signs that things are changing.

In February 2015, the U.S. Copyright Office released its "Copyright and the Music Marketplace Report," setting forth many suggestions for reforming outdated royalty rates and practices. The Department of Justice is considering major overhauls in the antiquated music licensing system. It may take a while to see improvements, and it could get worse before it gets better, but the conversation is in play.

This won't be the first time stakeholders have had to fight for their rights. And it probably won't be the last. All the way back in 1908, music publishers took issue with player pianos, because they mechanically recreated compositions without the manufacturer having to pay royalties. It took a lot of squeaky wheels, but Congress eventually compensated the creators for the unauthorized performances. So, we *have* prevailed before. The issues we face today make the matter of the player piano seem trivial, but the principle is the same: every new technological innovation creates challenges and a period of transition. The laws have to catch up. Hopefully, Congress will recognize that, once again, adjustments must be made.

Just about everyone, songwriters included, wants to see streaming succeed. Not only is it the way of the future, it has the potential to generate significant new revenue for an industry in disarray. Ironically, the very same digital technology that disrupted our business model could show us a workable way forward. I suspect it's not about fixing the old system but reinventing a brand new one.

Until then, it is my hope that policymakers, the tech world, and the songwriting community will be able to negotiate digital copyright law reform so that fair, transparent *distribution* of revenue will be a truly viable means of support for *all* parties involved. Wish us luck!

For a current status of these discussions, reviews and decisions please visit the "Getting Paid" page at www.ShellyPeiken.com.

****

On a more personal note, if I've inspired anyone to have a go at a new direction when staring bewilderedly at a *crossroads,* I say "go for it." I look forward to seeing you on the other side.

Thank you...

FROM THE MOMENT I made the decision to write this book I started meeting people who wanted to help me. I felt like I was being lifted above a crowd, passed from one set of good hands to another. I give my thanks.

To my Mom and Dad: I wish I could tell you.

First and foremost, thank you to Adam and Layla for giving me space and time. Extra thanks to my patient and generous husband Adam for his extensive pre-editing and helping me think things through at a time when he had plenty of other things he needed to do.

An abundance of thanks to my editor, agent, and new friend-for-life Ronny Schiff for appearing at the eleventh hour with her knowledge and experience and for pulling me past the finish line.

Much thanks to Alex Forbes for her expertise in proofreading and for her ongoing support and friendship.

Deep love and gratitude to Jesse Nash who believed in the book before I believed in it myself. To my 'wife,' Suzan Koç, for reading and fact checking and not getting tired of the stories she already knew too well. Thanks to David Wild for his generous foreword. To Kristen Graney for taking me by the hand and leading me down the social media rabbit hole and actually making it fun. To Nicole Powers for escorting me further down the rabbit hole, clearing images, and encouraging me to enjoy myself and ignore the analytics. To Lori Follett for her generosity and patience with a first time author. To Cindy Warden for reminding me to stay true.

Big love and thanks to (in order of their appearance on my journey) Mark Levinsohn, Kathleen Meyer, Allee Willis, Jeff Jampol, Jessica Bendinger, Julie Huey, Stéphanie Abou, Sarah Levin, Dan Kimpel, Peter Coquillard, Bennett Kaufman, Paul Doleman, Jamie Hartman, Jennifer Scott, Jason Leopold, Janis Schifter-Reemes, Brian Moreno, Cindy Meadors, Rose Gross-Marino, Peter Bliss, Eric Beall, Debra Baum, Denise Alvarado Collier, Amanda Slingerland, Aviad Cohen, Heidi Clements, Rachel Panchel, Yvette Corporon, Janette Billings Rich, Mark Cawley, Lisa Loeb, David Geha, Jim Rondinelli, Brad Parker, Laurie L. Hawkins, Lauren Grossman, Donna Cavanaugh, Karen Alpert, Mary Jo Braun, J. Charley Londoño, Jack Kugell, Elizabeth Abrams, Leslie Levine, Beth Nyland, Greg Fayer, Elliot Gipson, Marylee Ryan, Ali Young, Derek Baird, Jorge Hernandez, Doris Weinbaum, Karen Ray, John Meller, Mitchell Cohen, Ann Marie Gill, JoAnn Braheny, Liz Glotzer, Julie Kreiter.

Much appreciation to my Facebook friends who jumped onto my ride, joined in the conversations and kept me afloat with public and private messages of encouragement. You know who you are.

Glossary

A&R (Artist & Repertoire): A record label executive who signs talent and oversees all aspects of making a record. The music publishing community has taken on the term for their creative representatives as well, but for purposes of this book, it is used for label executives.

A capella: Without instrumental accompaniment.

Auto-Tune: A software program that can correct an out-of-tune vocal performance.

Backing Track: A pre-recorded musical bed of electronic and synthetic beats and sounds.

Billboard: An American music business trade publication that tracks and publishes charts of the most popular songs on a weekly basis, and features articles and columns on various aspects of the business.

Bridge: A transitional section of a song typically located before the final verse/chorus, which offers contrast before returning to the familiar refrain.

BVs (Background Vocals): Additional vocals, harmonic or otherwise, that compliment the melody.

Casting: The process of selecting the appropriate recording artists to whom a song is to be pitched.

Chi: Chinese term for the energy that surrounds us.

Cassette: A small plastic cartridge containing reel-to-reel magnetic tape (analog) used for recording, storing, and playback of music from the 1970s through the early 1990s.

CD (Compact Disc): A portable round disc used for recording, storing, and playback of music and data in digital form.

Chorus: The section of a song that recurs throughout as the main theme between the verses, usually featuring the "hook."

Comped: In regard to a recorded vocal, a composite of the most favorable lines, words, syllables so as to achieve the illusion of an optimum "one take" performance.

DAT (Digital Audio Tape): A small plastic tape cartridge used for recording, storing, and playback of digital data (as opposed to the then-prevailing analog tape) from the late 1980s through the 1990s.

Demo (Demonstration Tape): A model of what a fully-realized recording might sound like.

Demo Love: The condition of being so overly attached to the style in which a particular demo was presented that it inhibits the ability to adjust to a different stylistic approach.

East Rockaway: A village on New York's Long Island adjacent to the affluent "Five Towns."

EDM: Electronic dance music.

Finchel: The term for the relationship between Rachel Berry and Finn Hudson on the television program, "Glee."

Flip: A hairstyle made famous in the 1960s, characterized by straight hair with curled, turned-up ends.

Fluffers: An individual whose function is to get a male porn actor aroused before filming begins. In the context of this book: a backing track presented for the purpose of inspiring a topliner.

Frankenwriting: A large group of topliners who individually participate in the writing of a song with fragmented contributions.

Ghetto Blaster (aka Boombox): A large portable radio, cassette or CD player used for listening to music.

Greek life: A term used for fraternity and sorority culture on a college campus.

Hot 100: The weekly U.S. music industry chart published in *Billboard*, which tracks the popularity of singles.

Hook: Often found in the chorus of a song, it's a catchy, usually repetitive, turn of the melody and rhythm—an earworm.

Keppe: A Yiddish word for a baby's head.

Kvetched: A Yiddish word for complaining.

Mustela: A brand of baby soap.

Mitzvah: A Yiddish word for a good deed.

Plug-ins: Computer programs that augment an existing application in order to enhance its capability.

Pocket: The precise beat to which a word or phrase is sung.

Pro Tools: Digital audio workstation and recording software.

Producer: An individual who oversees the recording of an artist's song or album in the studio.

Pre-chorus (aka b-section, pre-hook, ramp, climb): The section of a song that occurs after the verse and heightens anticipation for the chorus.

Programmer: An individual who uses a computer or an electronic device to generate the sounds of musical instruments.

Satellite Radio: A commercial free, subscription digital service, broadcast primarily to cars from satellite.

Schmutz: Dirt; extraneous noise.

Single: A song that is "singled out" or chosen, usually from a larger collection and is released separately for sale, promotion or for commercial radio.

Soft Rhyme: Words that sound alike but are not an exact rhyme.

Synchronization Fee (or Sync Fee): The negotiated fee for the use of a music composition within some form of visual media.

Topline (noun): A millennial term for the melody and lyric, which is written for the purpose of accommodating a pre-existing or real time backing track.

Topline (verb—To topline; toplining): A millennial term for constructing a melody and lyric written for the purposes of accommodating a pre-existing or real time backing track.

Transistor Radio: The first pocket-sized portable radio, which used the transistor technology developed in the '50s and was wildly popular.

Verse: The parts of a song that introduce and develop the theme. There are usually two or three verses in a given song.

Y2K: A prediction that computer networks would crash and cause worldwide chaos when turning from 1999 to the year 2000.

Zeitgeist: The defining spirit of thought or mood of a particular period of history as modeled by the ideas and beliefs of the time.

Index of Songs

Index

Photograph, Text, and Lyric Credits

Every reasonable effort has been made to contact copyright holders and secure permissions. In the instances where this has not proved possible, we offer apologies to all concerned. Any omissions brought to our attention will be remedied in future editions.

Photograph Credits

At The Mint in L.A. Shelly with Kevin Griffin by Adam Gorgoni (Used by permission), 4; *Peiken family:* Personal collection, 10; *In My Room* by Leon Peiken, 12; *N.Y.C. Apt. #1 Ground floor* by Shelly Peiken, 14; *View from third floor, N.Y.C. Apt. #2* by Shelly Peiken, 15; *Shelly with Alexandra Forbes* by Mitch Young (Used by permission), 16; *My 12th Street landlord took me back. View from N.Y.C. Apt. #3* by Shelly Peiken, 21; *Shelly and Leon Peiken* by Celia Schwartz Pearl, 26; *Adam, 1991* by Shelly Peiken, 32; *Alannah Myles-style hair/blue contacts* by Mitch Young (Used by permission), 33; *Shelly and Jamie Weinman Marcus:* Personal collection, 34; *Adam on the futon* by Shelly Peiken, 42; *On the Boat* by Phil Roy (Used by permission), 45; *Kissing before SongSex. Carnie, Wendy and Glen* by Shelly Peiken, 49; *Corner of La Brea and Beverly* by Shelly Peiken, 54; *Bitch Video Shoot:* by Adam Gorgoni (Used by permission), 55; *Promotional spindle:* Personal collection, 56; *Ron Fair, Christina [Aguilera] and Shelly:* by Adam Gorgoni (Used by permission), 65; *That Wave* by Dale Swope (Used by permission), 68; *Washing Windows* (Used by permission of Digital Fortress Licensing and the *Baltimore Sun*), 69; *Layla and bottle* by Shelly Peiken, 71; *Napkin* by Shelly Peiken, 73; *Chrissie Hynde and Shelly* Personal collection, 76; *Sushi* by Shelly Peiken, 80; *Two Days in Cabo with Adam, Shelly, Kevin Cronin and Lisa Wells-Cronin:* Personal collection, 89; *Backstage with Christina:* by Dave Novik (Used by permission), 93; *Layla following an Olsen twin off the plane* by Shelly Peiken, 97; *Shower cap:* Selfie, 98; *Thinking twice about leaving* by Adam Gorgoni (Used by permission), 103; *Suzan Koç and Shelly:* Selfie, 108; *Sydelle Peiken* by Shelly Peiken, 110; *Layla and the Beatles* by Shelly Peiken (Beatles image used by permission, Apple Corps Ltd.), 116; *Shelly and Julian Lennon* by Suzan Koç (Used by permission), 121; *Dashboard* by Shelly Peiken, 125; *Pixelated poster:* Personal collection, 128; *If walls could talk...* by Ian Kirkpatrick (Used by permission), 136; *Layla and Miley Cyrus* by Shelly Peiken, 140;

Layla and David Archuleta by Shelly Peiken, 141; *Layla and Jesse McCartney* by Shelly Peiken, 141; *Greg Wells and Natasha Bedingfield* by Shelly Peiken, 147; *Mozella* by Becca Surowiec Tibus (Used by permission), 150; *Plain White T's* by Matt Harris (Used by permission), 152; *Miles Copeland hosted a retreat at his castle…* by Mark Cawley (Used by permission), 173; *Adam Anders and Peer Aström on Skype* by Shelly Peiken, 175; *Shelly, Javier Colon and Xandy Barry* by Wally Gagel (Used by permission), 188; *Wedding Day* by Layla Gorgoni (Used by permission), 191; *Katharine McPhee and Shelly* by Ian Kirkpatrick (Used by permission), 194; *Shelly and Adam* [Grammy photo] by Jim McHugh (Used by permission), 216; *Grammy Party* by Dan Petel (Used by permission), 219; *Layla and car* by Shelly Peiken, 221; *Carpool:* Selfie (Used with permission of passengers), 225; *Screenshot of Layla's text* courtesy of Shelly's iPhone, 227; *Jesse Nash and Shelly:* Personal collection, 231; *Chris Mann* by Dana Patrick (Used by permission), 234; *The Rolling Stones with Keith Urban* by Kevin Mazur (Used by permission of Getty Images); *Shelly:* Selfie, 237; *Ruth [Anderson-Davis] and Shelly:* Personal collection, 246; *Allee Willis* by Justin Sullivan (Used by permission), 252; *Layla in pink dress* by Adam Gorgoni (Used by permission), 254; *Author photo* by Moni Vargas (Used by Permission), 257

Literary/Film Quotes

"Serial" definition by Shelly Peiken.

Excerpt from *The Shawshank Redemption,* granted courtesy of Warner Bros. Entertainment Inc.

Excerpt from *The Places That Scare You,* by Pema Chödrön, © 2001 by Pema Chödrön. Reprinted by arrangement with The Permissions Company, Inc., on behalf of Shambhala Publications, Inc., www.shambhala.com.

Letter from Ruth Anderson-Davis, used by permission of Ruth Anderson-Davis.

Lyric Credits

"Almost Doesn't Count" Words and Music by Shelly Peiken and Guy Roche. Copyright © 1998, 1999 Sushi Too Music (BMI) and Manuniti L.A. All rights for Sushi Too Music (BMI) administered by Kobalt Music Publishing America, Inc. All Rights Reserved. International Copyright Secured. Used by Permission.

"Bitch" Words and Music by Meredith Brooks and Shelly Peiken. Copyright © 1996, 1997 Sushi Too Music (BMI), EMI Blackwood Music Inc., Kissing Booth Music Inc., and Warner-Tamerlane Publishing Corp. All rights for Kissing Booth Music Inc. controlled and administered by EMI Blackwood Music Inc. All rights for Sushi Too Music (BMI) administered by Kobalt Music Publishing America, Inc. All Rights Reserved. International Copyright Secured. Used by Permission.

"Boys of Summer, The" Words and Music by Don Henley and Mike W. Campbell. Copyright © 1984 Woody Creek Music and Wild Gator Music, All Rights for Woody Creek Music Administered by WB Music Corp. All Rights Reserved. *Reprinted by Permission of Alfred Music Publishing.*

"Carry Your Heart" Words and Music by Shelly Peiken. Copyright © 1987 Sydelleon Songs (BMI). Administered by Kobalt Music Publishing America, Inc. All Rights Reserved. International Copyright Secured. Used by Permission.

"Creep" Words and Music by Albert Hammond, Mike Hazlewood, Thomas Yorke, Jonathan Greenwood, Colin Greenwood, Edward O'Brien and Philip Selway. Copyright © 1992 EMI April Music Inc., Warner/Chappell Music Ltd., and Imagem Songs Limited. All Rights for Warner/Chappell Music Ltd. in the U.S. and Canada Administered by WB Music Corp. All Rights Reserved. International Copyright Secured. Used by Permission—contains elements of "The Air That I Breathe" by Albert Hammond and Mike Hazlewood, Copyright © 1972 EMI April Music Inc. *Reprinted by Permission of Hal Leonard Corporation.*

About the Author

GRAMMY-NOMINATED SONGWRITER SHELLY Peiken has been a prolific, behind-the-scenes force in the music business for more than two decades. Her songs have sold in excess of 50 million records. She is best known for penning culturally resonant, female-empowerment anthems such as Christina Aguilera's No. 1 hit, "What a Girl Wants" and Meredith Brooks' smash, "Bitch."

Shelly's experiences, accomplishments and the circles in which she has traveled give her a unique perspective on the music business: that of a professional woman who fought her way into a highly competitive industry, found a way to succeed, balanced a thriving career and a family, and who has witnessed firsthand the changes that have turned that industry upside down. All the while, Shelly has stayed true to her first true love: the often elusive but always immensely satisfying act of writing a great song.